W9-BRU-422

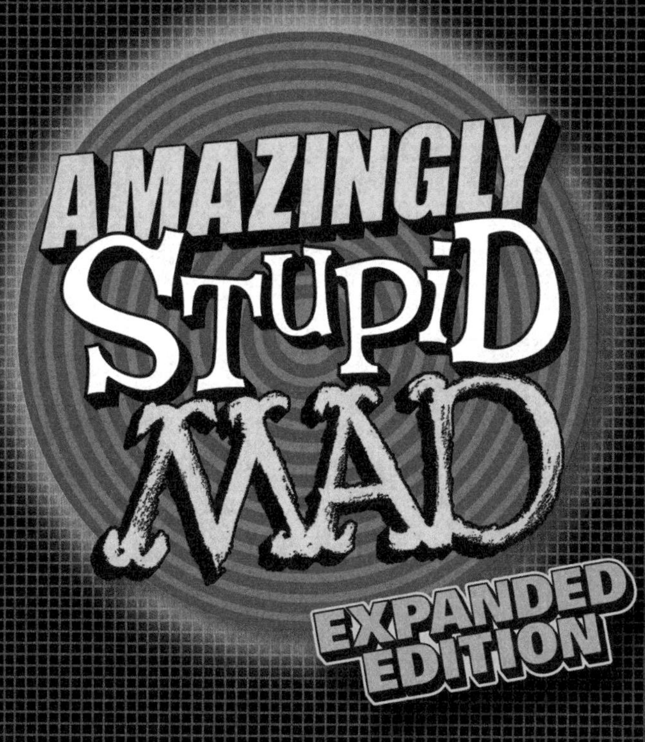
AMAZINGLY
STUPID
MAD
EXPANDED
EDITION

BY "THE USUAL GANG OF IDIOTS"

FALL RIVER PRESS
New York

FALL RIVER PRESS

New York

An Imprint of Sterling Publishing
387 Park Avenue South
New York, NY 10016

This 2013 compilation published by Fall River Press, by arrangement with MAD Books.

Contents of this compilation appeared originally in slightly different form in
Amazingly Stupid MAD and *Epic MAD*.

ISBN 978-1-4351-5175-8

Distributed in Canada by Sterling Publishing
C/o Canadian Manda Group, 165 Dufferin Street
Toronto, Ontario, Canada M6K 3H6

For information about custom editions, special sales, and premium and corporate purchases, please contact Sterling Special Sales at 800-805-5489 or specialsales@sterlingpublishing.com.

Manufactured in the United States of America

2 4 6 8 10 9 7 5 3

www.sterlingpublishing.com

CONTENTS

SPIDER-M

WAITER! ! There's a **FLY** in my soup! !

THHLOR

SPRIZZITZ

WHIR
WHIR
WHIR
WHIR

SKROINCH

AN FUNNIES

WRITER AND ARTIST: DON MARTIN

A COLLECTION OF VITAL TEMPERATURE READINGS

...is the lowest the temperature is when your air conditioner konks out.

...is the temperature of the average toilet seat on the average Winter morning.

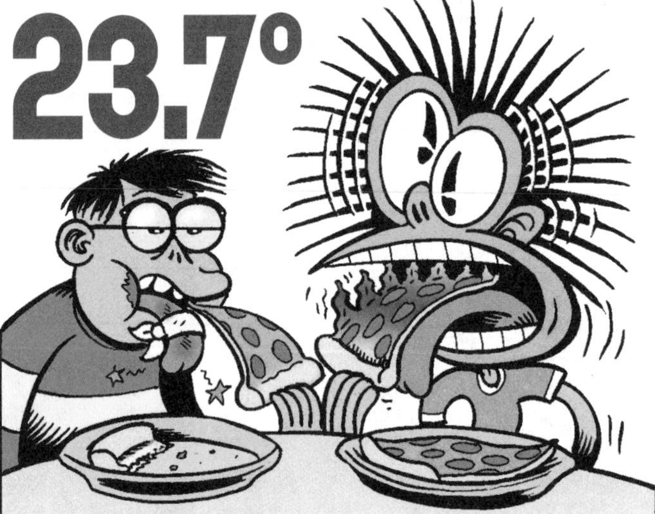

...is the difference in temperature between your first and second slices of pizza.

100
80
60
40
20

...is how much warmer the kiddie wading pool always is compared to the adult pool.

WRITER: J. PRETE ARTIST: PETER BAGGE

FOUND ON THE MAD THERMOMETER

103.7°

...is your temperature when your Mother finally announces to the world, "I think it's time we called the Doctor!"

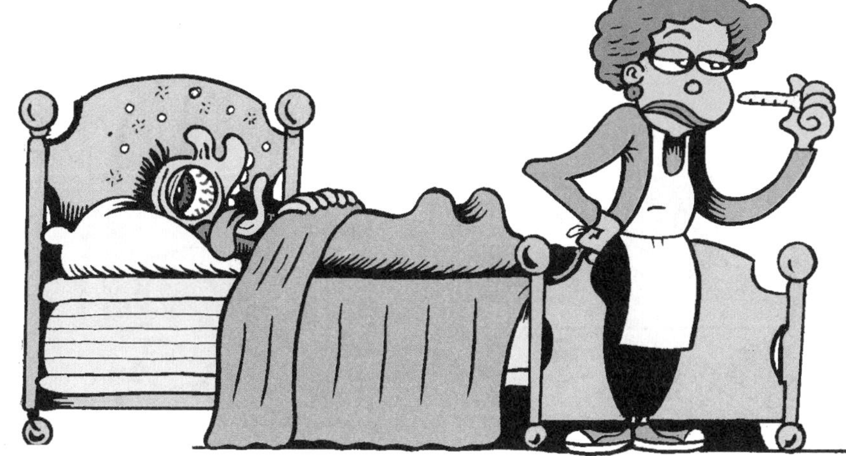

110°

...is the temperature of your dog's breath whenever he pants over you while you're sleeping.

9°

...is the average temperature of your Doctor's stethoscope when he tries to examine you.

75.5°

...is the temperature when the chewing gum stuck to the bottom of your school desk starts to get yecchy again.

34.4°

...is the hottest those artificial heating lamps will ever keep fast-food French fries.

104.5°

...is the minimum the temperatur[e] must be for your Mother to let you step foot out of the house without saying, "Take a sweater for later on!"

92.6°

...and humid is the temperature when the tape holding up your posters gives out.

212°

...was the temperature in your fish tank the night the electric heater went haywir[e]

JOKE AND DAGGER DEPT.

WRITER AND ARTIST: ANTONIO PROHIAS COLORIST: CARRIE STRACHAN

THE PLAYGROUND OF KIDS YOUR PA
Children Who've Knocked Their Eyes Out Playing With Pea Shooters, BB Guns, Rubber Bands and Paper Clips, Paper Airplanes or Any Item Not Made of Foam Rubber.
The Boy Whose Face Remained Frozen After He Made One Too Many Funny Faces.
The Girl Whose Hair-do Literally Caused Her Parents to Die of Shame.
POLICE
WRITER: BARRY LIEBMANN ARTIST: TOM BUNK

NTS ALWAYS TELL YOU ABOUT
BUT YOU'VE NEVER SEEN YOURSELF!!!
The Girl Whose Ears Were So Dirty That Vegetables Were Growing Out of Them.
V8
The Foreign Child Whose Existence Somehow Depended Upon Whether or Not You Finished All Your Creamed Broccoli.
DIET
WINE
The Sixth Grader Who Played a Rock Album Backwards and Instantly Became a Satan Worshipper.
THIS SIDE UP
I ♥ NY
TOM BUNK
The Seven-Year Old Whose Life Was Destroyed Because of Bad Marks on His Permanent Record.

A MAD LOOK AT

WRITER AND ARTIST: SERGIO ARAGONÉS

WHEN YOU WISH UPON A CAR DEPT.

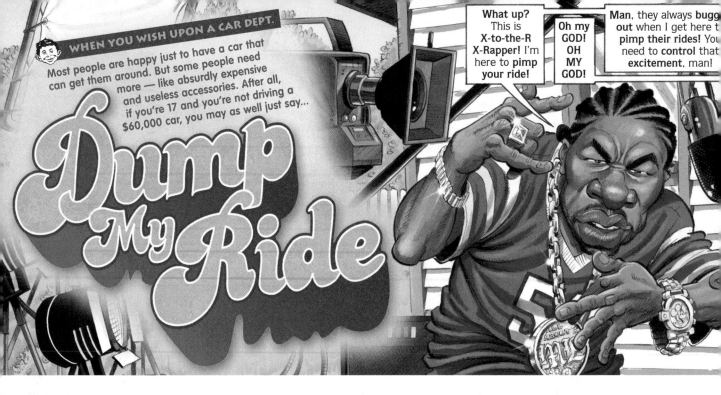

Most people are happy just to have a car that can get them around. But some people need more — like absurdly expensive and useless accessories. After all, if you're 17 and you're not driving a $60,000 car, you may as well just say...

Dump My Ride

What up? This is **X-to-the-R X-Rapper!** I'm here to **pimp your ride!**

Oh my GOD! OH MY GOD!

Man, they always **bugg out** when I get here t **pimp their rides!** You need to **control** that **excitement**, man!

citement?!? Try terror! I saw some thugged-out black dude sniffing round my car, then making his way my walk! I'm just trying to defend nyself until the cops can get here!

Aw, quit frontin', man! Everyone acts so shocked — like you didn't notice me and my camera crew setting up on your front lawn for the last two hours!
SWEET

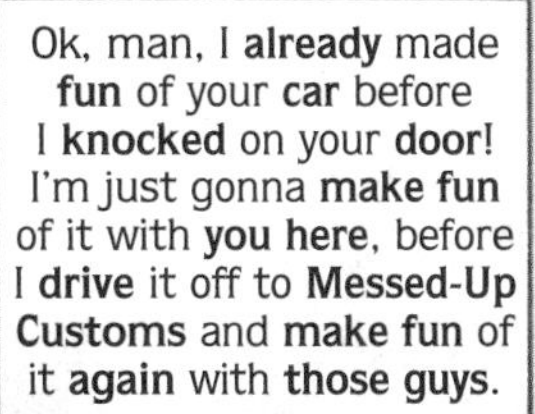

Ok, man, I already made fun of your car before I knocked on your door! I'm just gonna make fun of it with you here, before I drive it off to Messed-Up Customs and make fun of it again with those guys.

That's not exactly biting satire, man! The whole point of the show is that I realize my ride is beat! Hey, maybe you can get a job hosting The Swan so you can point out to the contestants that they're fugly!

ARTIST: TOM RICHMOND WRITER: DAVE CROATTO

What are you even laughing at? And can you at least make eye contact with me?
I laugh at all my own lame cracks! Hyuh! Hyuh! It's either that or my deadpan look of disbelief!

This better?
Just take the car and go!

ood work, guys! Now we e time to give the viewers at they really want to see: e prop comedy that would ke even Carrot Top cringe!
That's BULL!

When you brought your wheels in here, your trunk was cluttered with all kinds of junk — a spare tire, a jack, flares... so we decided to convert your trunk into a slot car track!
Your solution to my messy trunk was to give me a useless trunk?

No — 'cause check this out! The geniuses at Messed-Up Customs also gave you a trailer hitch and this U-Haul! Problem solved!
U-HAUL
50

And we added a 40-inch hanging plasma screen TV so your friends could watch all that scale-model racing action!
Wow, I don't have that nice a TV in my house!
Well, this is even better, my man — 'cause now you can watch it while standing with a bunch of people in your driveway or in a parking lot!

So, uh, where's my spare now?
Dude, when you get a flat, you're gonna have to replace a $400 customized Pirelli racing tire! Where your spare's at is the *least* of your problems!

And listen up — that trunk monitor is just the beginning! Behind every rim, we mounted a 13-inch plasma screen TV! That's four monitors that no one will be able to see! But you'll know they're there — and that's pimped!
We even hooked up TiVo, so you can see the shows you missed, if you're not in your car for some crazy reason!
Plus, we added a monitor behind every headrest, another one in the dash, along with an MP4 player! Plus two PlayStations in the back and a T-Mobile Sidekick II mounted right into your steering wheel! Now you'll never be stuck watching that boring road again!

Now, we know you love junk food like French fries and corndogs and that stuff!
Yeah, I do!
So we worked your passion right into your ride! We dropped a custom "Fry Daddy 4000" right where your passenger seat used to be! Now you can deep-fry while you drive!
Is that safe?
There's gonna be some splattering — but we hooked you up with these gloves! They match your paint job!

Thanks everyone! X-Rapper, *Messed-Up Customs* — this car is totally going to change my life!

Later that day... when the show is finished filming...

After I left **Messed-Up Customs**, I was **hungry**, so I decided to hit **McDonald's**. There, I held up the **line** at the **drive-thru** for **20 minutes**, struggling to get **free** of the stupid **racing harness** so I could pay the **cashier**!
SWEET
PLEASE PAY HERE

The guy **behind me** in line was watching the **monitors** in my **headrest** and ended up **rear-ending** me — completely destroying my **Waterford Crystal bumper!**
CRUNCH!

And, although it's definitely "**pimped**," it turns out that **airbags** made from **stitched-together $20 bills** aren't that **effective**!

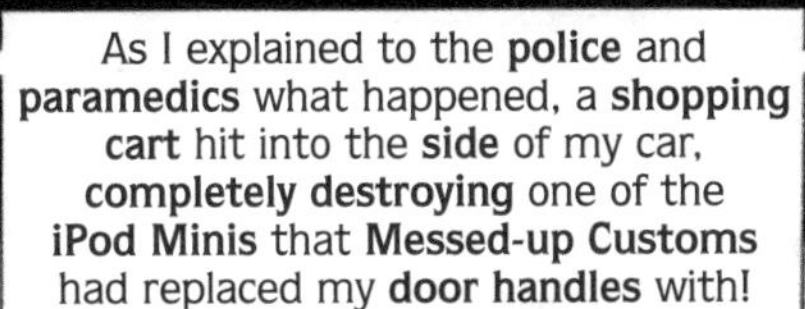

As I finally pulled through, a **homeless** guy **squeegeed** my **windshield** and some of the **soapy water** got under the **ood**, shorting out the **mother-board** for my **electronics**!
As I explained to the **police** and **paramedics** what happened, a **shopping cart** hit into the **side** of my car, **completely destroying** one of the **iPod Minis** that **Messed-up Customs** had replaced my **door handles** with!

I **finally** got **out** of there, and headed over to my **friend's** to show off my **ride**! But when I went over the **train tracks**, I **bottomed out**, causing the **koi fish** to come out of their **backseat pond**, and **ruining** the **cashmere carpeting** in the process!
BIG PIMPN

I **realized** that with all the **stuff** I was **powering**, I now got about **three miles** to the **gallon**! I had to **stop** to **clean out** all the **fish corpses** anyway, so I pulled into a **gas station**. While trying to fill up my **wiper fluid**, I accidentally put it in the engine-mounted **coffee maker!**

After a quick **stomach-pumping** at the **hospital**, I went to pick up a bunch of **friends** — and almost **drowned** two of them after **forgetting** to drain the **koi pond** first!

I **parked** at the **mall** and when I came back **out**, my **ride** was **gutted**! I guess, having **$20,000** worth of **electronics** in **plain sight** isn't the best **anti-theft device**!
Thanks again, Messed-Up Customs!

CARDS for SOMEONE who's having a BAD DAY

Sharing the Pain You're Feeling

You bragged about how tough you are
And thought that it was cool;
And soon your mighty fighting words
Were heard throughout the school;
If only you had been concerned
By what you said more fully,
You might have saved yourself from getting
Creamed by the school bully.

ARTIST: JOHN CALDWELL

ARTIST: CHARLES AKINS

Sorry For Your Loss

Your life's an endless struggle
And the world does not seem fair
And often you're tormented by
The darkness of despair;
Deep sorrows fill your heart with grie
This cannot be denied;
But none can match your sadness
When your iPod crashed and died.

Such a Pity

At school you felt the urge to poop,
But as all students know,
The bathrooms are a filthy mess
And so you didn't go;
But then the urge grew stronger
And you prayed that you could shake it;
Your house is just a block away—
Next time we hope you'll make it.

ARTIST: BOB STAAKE

ARTIST: RICH POWELL

Thinking of You

You wolf down hot dogs by the ton,
Pig out on shakes and fries;
They know you well at Burger King,
Which comes as no surprise;
But yesterday you went too far
And now must take the rap;
Not only did you barf in class
But in the teacher's lap.

WRITER: FRANK JACOBS

In Your Time of Embarrassment

The sound of farting fills the room;
The stink no one can bear;
And now it's you your classmates blame;
They point at you and stare;
You sit there while they shout your name;
"You farted!" they remind you;
Which really stinks, because it was
The kid who sits behind you!

In This Time of Sadness

You once enjoyed those hearty meals
Of chicken, ham and beef,
But now each night at supper time
Your life is filled with grief;
Your mom's turned vegetarian,
Small wonder that you're sad;
Thank goodness that you own a dog —
Hey, Alpo ain't half-bad!

Understanding During This Difficult Period

Your friends are looking closely
At your recent dental work;
We're sure it's not a pleasure
When you see them laugh and smirk;
Most sadly, you cannot forget
Those looks upon their faces,
When yesterday you tried to eat
Spaghetti — wearing braces.

A VISIT TO THE COUNTRY

BREET-BREET TOOD TOOD

BREET-BREET TOOD TOOD

We find it **quite restful!**

D. MARTIN

DEVICE AGE DEPT.

WHAT IF TECHNOLOGY

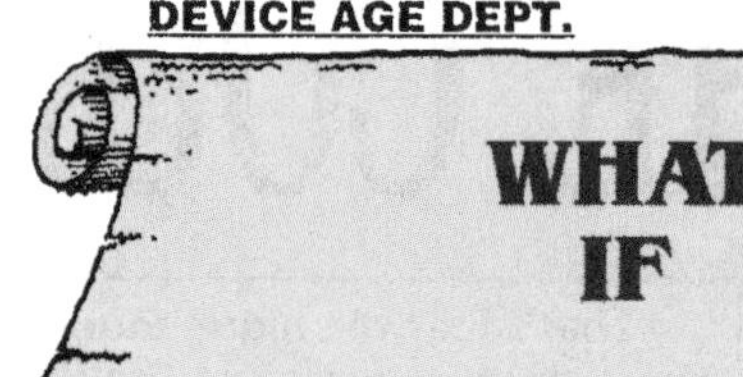

What if Moses had a Fax Machine!

What if Alexander Graham Bell had Call Waiting!

What if Medieval Knights had Refrigerator Magnets!

VADED **HISTORY?!?**

ARTIST AND WRITER: JOHN CALDWELL

What if Adam and Eve had Post-It Notes!

What if Vincent Van Gogh had a Walkman!

What if Nero had a Karaoke Machine!

What if Paul Revere had a Pager!

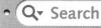

Planet TAD!!!!!

http://www.galaxyo'blogs.com/planettad  Search

Planet TAD!!!!!

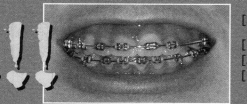

[**About Me**]

[**Name**|Tad]
[**Age**|14]
[**Middle name**|
None of your business]

[31 October|**08:41pm**]

[**mood**| full of tiny Snickers bars]

Tonight was Halloween, and my little sister Sophie decided to go as an angel. When I saw her downstairs in the hallway, I pointed out that "angel" is one possible name for her costume. Another is "dead kid." And then Sophie started crying and went to her room and wouldn't come out, and Mom and Dad made me go to my room.

[2 November|**07:34pm**]

I just finished the sixth Harry Potter book, and here's what I don't understand about Hogwarts: Okay, so, the school has a sorting hat that can figure out each student's true nature, and assign him to the appropriate house, right? But there are four houses. Three of them — Gryffindor, Hufflepuff, and Ravenclaw — are full of normal people. And then there's Slytherin, which is NOTHING BUT EVIL PEOPLE. If I ran Hogwarts, when the sorting hat assigned a student to Slytherin, I'd send him home, or maybe to, like, wizard reform school. I mean, duh.

[4 November|**04:15pm**]

At school today, the signs went up for the fall dance, Pilgrimfest '05. (It's called Pilgrimfest because it happens around Thanksgiving. They decorate the gym with leaves and cutouts of turkeys.) I've decided to ask Katie Zembla from my geometry class. She seems really friendly and pretty, and she's always really nice to me after I let her copy my homework.

[7 November|**03:37pm**]

[**mood**|  feeling dorky]

I tried asking Katie to the dance today, but I got all nervous and wound up asking to borrow her eraser instead. And then I had to erase

[**mood**| feeling completely dorky]

I tried asking Katie again, but I wound up asking her to borrow her protractor. It's getting embarrassing.

[9 November|**05:05pm**]

[**mood**| very happy]

Good news! I finally asked her, and she said she'd go with me! Well, actually, she said she'd go if this person she's waiting to ask her doesn't by Friday. So I'm her second choice!

[11 November|**03:36pm**]

It's Friday, and I caught up with Katie after class, and she says he still hasn't asked her, but she wants to give him until Monday.

[14 November|**04:10pm**]

[**mood**| very very very very happy]

Hooray! Katie said she'd go with me! Pilgrimfest is four days away, so I have until then to find out stuff like what to wear and how to dance.

[16 November|**06:51pm**]

Mom took me to the mall today to look for a new tie. I like the one I have, but she says girls don't like boys who like ties that look like fish.

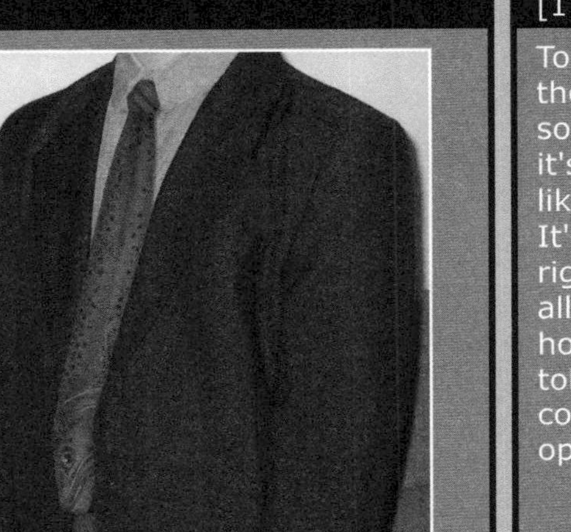

[17 November|**07:18pm**]

Tomorrow's the big dance! I went to the Dollar Depot today and bought some cK One cologne. Well, actually, it's called dB Two, but it smells just like cK One, and it only costs a buck! It's pretty good — my dad noticed it right when he came home, and I was all the way up in my room. He asked how much I paid for it, and when I told him, he said, "That's a bargain for cologne that strong!" And then he opened all the windows.

[19 November|**11:26am**]

[**mood**| itchy]

Ugh. I didn't wind up going to the dance after all. I woke up yesterday morning covered in hives. Mom took me to Dr. Bauer, who tested me and told me that I'm probably allergic to the artificial musk in the dB Two, which I guess is good to know. He gave me some Benadryl, and I spent the night at home, recovering, watching TV with my parents. They tried to be nice about it, but every once in a while, my dad would look over at me and start laughing, and then he'd try to pretend that he was laughing at the TV, but we were watching Law & Order SVU, which isn't really all that funny.

ARTIST: BRIAN DURNIAK WRITER: TIM CARVELL

A MAD LOOK AT THE MOMENT BEFORE THE DISASTER

KEEP
OFF
THE GRASS
PORGES

THE CONTINUING ADVENTURES OF WILLY NILLY

Cents-Less Coupons

your money-saving circular

Surprise! That's NOT Meat! It's Mulch, Mulch More.

Taste familiar? It should.
Your old comic books are in there. So's your baseball card collection. (Thanks, Mom!) Grass clippings, too. And so's the oak that came down in that storm last March and blocked the street until a road crew could get out with a chainsaw and a wood chipper! It's *all* in there, plus a lot more. With Fiber Burger, a meatless patty made from recycled materials isn't pulp fiction anymore.

Fiber Burger

85% Post-Consumer Content 100% Delicious

MANUFACTURER'S COUPON	NOT REDEEMABLE

Save $1.00

on any variety of *Fiber Burger*

TO THE CONSUMER: This coupon is good on any purchase of FIBER BURGER Recycled Meal Patties. Any other use constitutes fraud. It's a lousy coupon! What else are you going to do with it?! Pay off a gambling debt? Re-paper the bedroom? Collect your dry-cleaning? Listen, pal, it's not worth it. You've worked too hard to get where you are to throw it all away like this. Think of your family, man! There's people out there who care about you! It doesn't have to end this way. C'mon, now, drop the coupon. That's it. Nice and slowly...Okay, Becker, MOVE IN NOW! GO GO GO!

TRY ALL 4 VARIETIES!

Hickory Newsprint

Pepper Maché

Spicy Cardboard & Crabgrass

Kinko's™ Smokehouse

PHOTOGRAPHER: IRVING SCHILD WRITER: SCOTT MAIKO

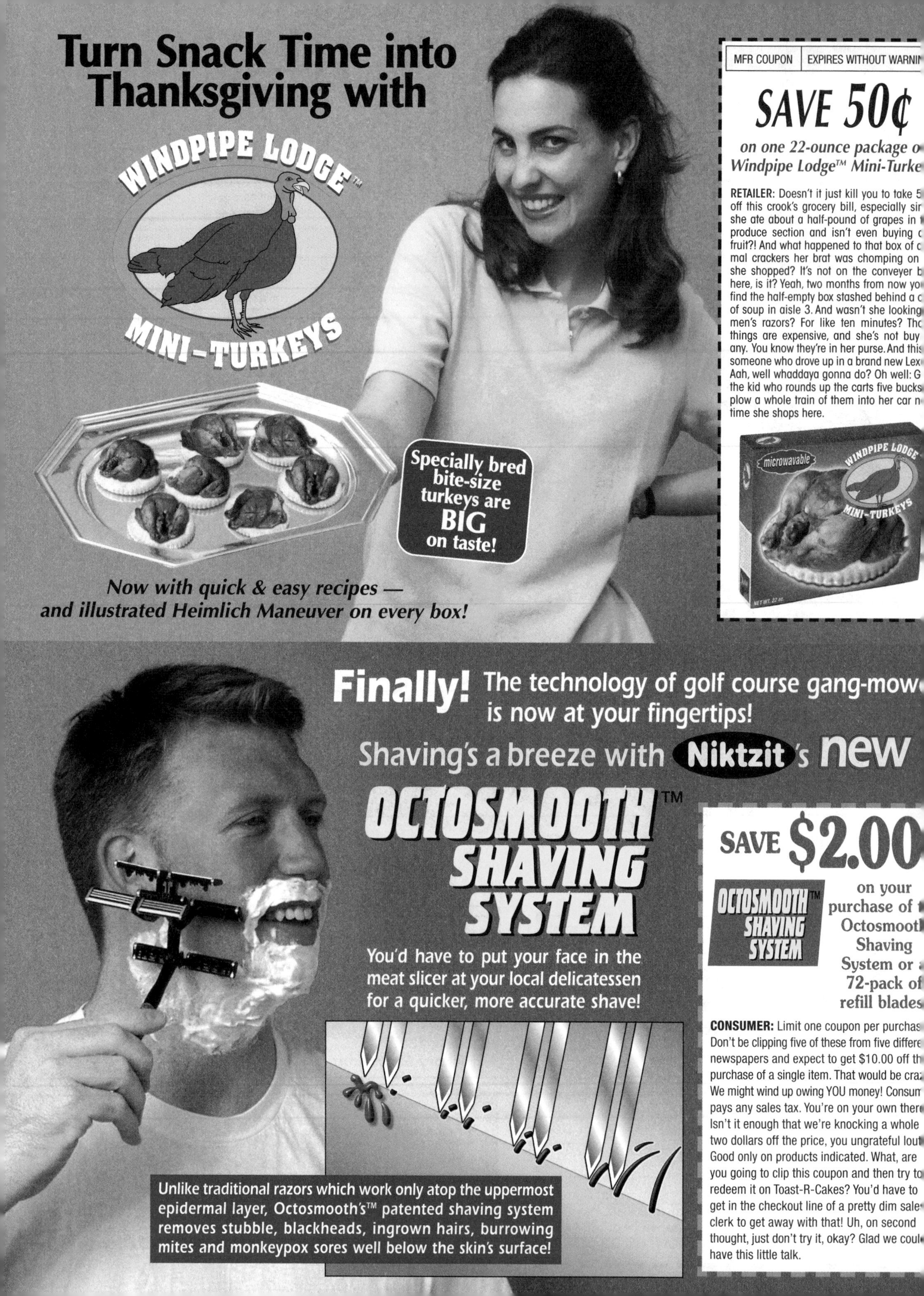

Turn Snack Time into Thanksgiving with

WINDPIPE LODGE™
MINI-TURKEYS

Specially bred bite-size turkeys are BIG on taste!

Now with quick & easy recipes —
and illustrated Heimlich Maneuver on every box!

MFR COUPON | EXPIRES WITHOUT WARNI

SAVE 50¢

on one 22-ounce package o
Windpipe Lodge™ Mini-Turke

RETAILER: Doesn't it just kill you to take 5 off this crook's grocery bill, especially sir she ate about a half-pound of grapes in t produce section and isn't even buying c fruit?! And what happened to that box of c mal crackers her brat was chomping on she shopped? It's not on the conveyer b here, is it? Yeah, two months from now yo find the half-empty box stashed behind a c of soup in aisle 3. And wasn't she looking men's razors? For like ten minutes? Th things are expensive, and she's not buy any. You know they're in her purse. And this someone who drove up in a brand new Lex Aah, well whaddaya gonna do? Oh well: G the kid who rounds up the carts five bucks plow a whole train of them into her car n time she shops here.

Finally! The technology of golf course gang-mow is now at your fingertips!

Shaving's a breeze with Niktzit's new

OCTOSMOOTH™ SHAVING SYSTEM

You'd have to put your face in the meat slicer at your local delicatessen for a quicker, more accurate shave!

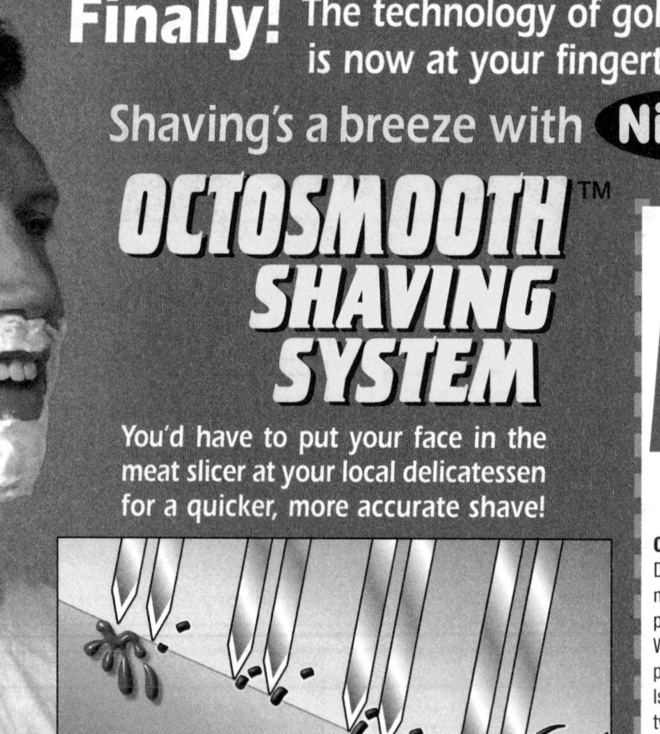

Unlike traditional razors which work only atop the uppermost epidermal layer, Octosmooth's™ patented shaving system removes stubble, blackheads, ingrown hairs, burrowing mites and monkeypox sores well below the skin's surface!

SAVE $2.00

OCTOSMOOTH™ SHAVING SYSTEM

on your purchase of t Octosmoot Shaving System or 72-pack of refill blades

CONSUMER: Limit one coupon per purchas Don't be clipping five of these from five differe newspapers and expect to get $10.00 off th purchase of a single item. That would be craz We might wind up owing YOU money! Consum pays any sales tax. You're on your own there Isn't it enough that we're knocking a whole two dollars off the price, you ungrateful lout Good only on products indicated. What, are you going to clip this coupon and then try to redeem it on Toast-R-Cakes? You'd have to get in the checkout line of a pretty dim sale clerk to get away with that! Uh, on second thought, just don't try it, okay? Glad we coul have this little talk.

"Finally... A bubble gum for my dog!"
DOG-BLO
Flavored Bubble Gum For Dogs
Six Fun Flavors to Choose From!
Rawhide
Table Scraps
Antifreeze
Rotted Meat
Spearmint Poinsettia
Expensive Leather Shoe
DOG-BLO BUBBLE GUM FOR DOGS
RAWHIDE FLAVOR
MANUFACTURER'S COUPON
EXPIRES NOON, TUESDAY
Save 10¢
on a single pack of
DOG-BLO
Bubble Gum for Dogs
Consumer: If you expect to find this product next time you go to the supermarket, you'll be in for a big surprise. If you don't believe us, try looking for it. Go up and down the pet food aisle — more than once. Is that it next to the cat litter? We don't think so! Do it about three or four times. By then you'll be so tired you won't even care that we're going to shout "Told you so! Told you so!" when you let us know we were right all along. Spend your time picking out a box of cereal instead.

ROAMING WASN'T BILLED IN A DAY DEPT.

Consider a cell phone plan that gives you 500 free minutes a month. 500 minutes! Not 300, not 400...500!! That's sooo many minutes! That is, until you start using them the way a lot of cell phone owners do — then 500 isn't so many minutes! Need proof? Just review the findings of our exhaustively researched and lavishly illustrated study we call...

MAD'S FEARLESS BREAK-DOWN OF 500 FREE CELL PHONE MINUTES

15 minutes:

Calling someone you're in the same room with as a joke.

8 minutes:

At a restaurant, saying the same nine words over and over again...

33 minutes:

Making long distance calls to people you wouldn't otherwise talk to if you had to pay long distance charges.

3 minutes:

Calling in your pizza order from the parking lot after determining that the line was too long to wait on.

26 minutes:

Calling home to ask what you were sent to the store for.

18 minutes:

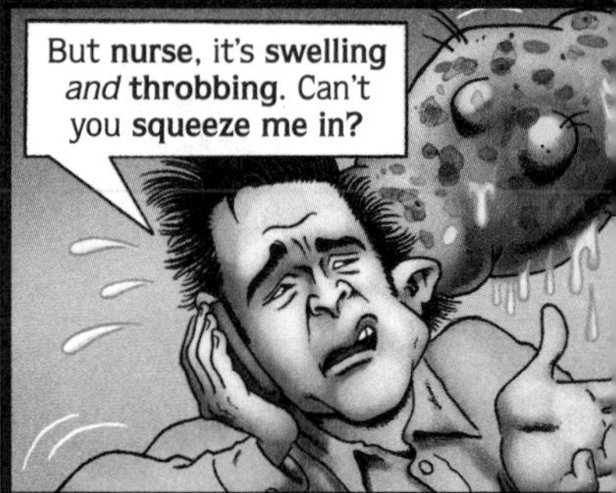

Calling around for a good brain tumor doctor.

16 minutes:

Calling your own number and pretend to be talking to someone to avoid hav to talk to someone who's with you.

21 minutes:

Getting or giving "real time" driving directions.

ARTIST: RICK TULKA
COLORIST: CARRIE STRACHAN
WRITER: BUTCH D'AMBROSIO

minutes:

lling your boyfriend or girlfriend to all you at home so you don't use up all of your minutes.

16 minutes:

Pretending that your connection is breaking up to people you don't want to talk to anymore.

0 minutes:

An actual emergency.

0 minutes:

Listening to your favorite TV show by having somebody at home hold the phone up to the set.

10 minutes:

Wasted while trying to get your "hands free" earpiece to stay in your ear.

39 minutes:

Navigating the automated customer service menu to find out how many minutes you have left.

2 minutes:

eturning a dropped call only to find at neither you nor the person you're lling back has anything more to say.

43 minutes:

On a road trip, talking to friends in the car in front of you.

2 minutes:

Having a celebrity you ran into tell your mother "Hi."

5 minutes:

Asking, "Can you hear me?"

75 minutes:

Saying, "I can't hear you."

19 minutes:

Making arrangements to switch over to a competitor's phone plan with 1,000 free minutes included.

Just pick a different item from each row as you read your way down the page and you'll have a zany new Naruto episode every time!

MAKE YOUR OWN NUTTY NARUTO EPISODE!

WRITER: KENT PARKER
ARTIST: STEVE SMALLWOOD

NARUTO  | SAKURA  | SASUKE  | AKAMARU  | KIBA  | ROCK LEE  | TENTEN  | INO

USES

SHADOW CLONE JUTSU

PB&J SANDWICHES

A WHOOPEE CUSHION

A SUPER SOAKER

TRUE LOVE

A PLAYSTATION 3

DENTAL FLOSS

KETCHUP PACKETS

TO FIGHT

HAKU

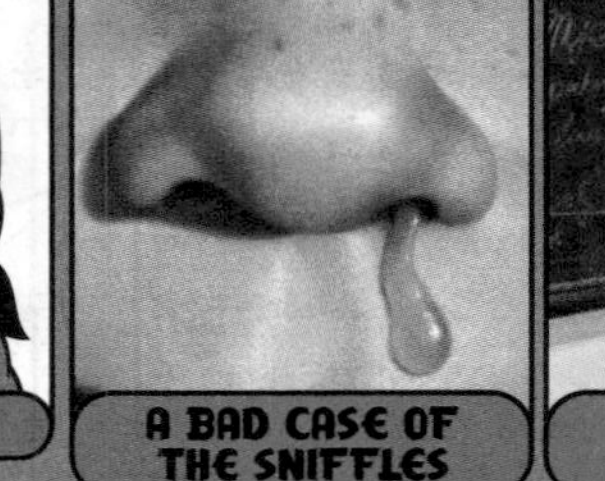

A BAD CASE OF THE SNIFFLES

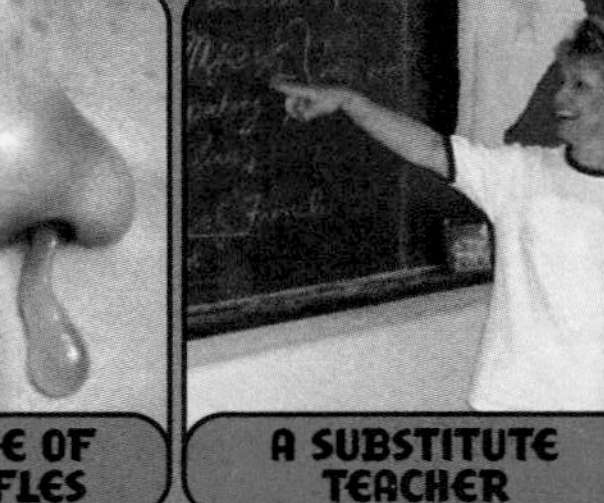

A SUBSTITUTE TEACHER

BARNEY

THE EVIL COUNT OLAF

TONY HAWK

SPAM

AN UNFAIR BEDTIME

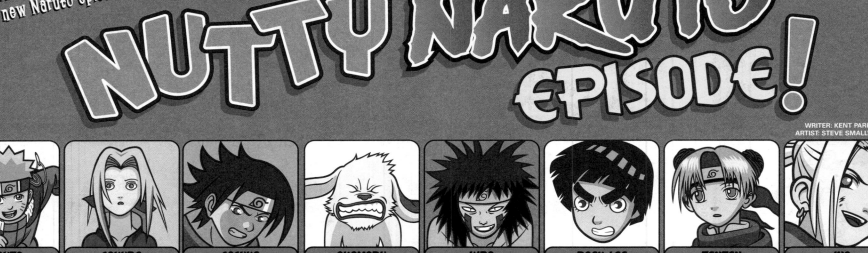

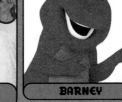

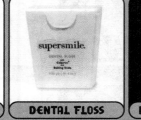

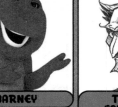

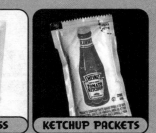

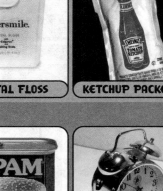

KAKASHI
AANG
DANNY PHANTOM
SONIC THE HEDGEHOG
SCOOBY-DOO
CHUCK E. CHEESE
JACK BLACK
THE CAST OF HIGH SCHOOL MUSICAL
BATTLES
ZABUZA
PLANKTON
TOOTH DECAY
A BAND OF PIRATES
JESSE MCCARTNEY
POISON IVY
A FERRET
A PARKING TICKET
AND THEN RESCUES
HINATA
YOUR BABY SISTER
THE SPELLING BEE FINALISTS
JAMIE LYNN SPEARS
BILLY AND MANDY
LANCE ARMSTRONG
LIGHTNING MCQUEEN
ED & EDD BUT NOT EDDY
FROM
OROCHIMARU
THE SCHOOL LUNCH LADY
A TISSUE FULL OF FRESH BOOGERS
DARTH TATER
A SWARM OF BEES
A NATIONWIDE TOILET PAPER SHORTAGE
A CRAZED DENTIST
A CONFUSED LION TAMER
JUST IN TIME TO RETURN HOME TO
TAKE THE CHUNIN EXAM
MAKE SPAGHETTI
RETURN OVERDUE LIBRARY BOOKS
DO LAUNDRY
CATCH THE CW'S FALL LINEUP
GO POTTY
MOW THE LAWN
SNAP INTO A SLIM JIM

ONE FINE DAY AT A BANK

WRITER: DON EDWING ARTIST: DON MARTIN

Harry Potter may be the biggest thing in publishing right now – but it's certainly not the *smartest.* Although the series has made tons of money, J.K. Rowling has repeatedly stated that the saga would only be seven books long. That's no way to do business! Fellow children's author Lemony Snicket, however, knows that the secret to success is to find a formula, stick with it, and above all else, never take *any* steps to resolve the plot and kill that golden goose! Just turn this magazine sideways and read on – maybe then you'll understand what keeps the kids interested (and shelling out their parents' bucks), all for...

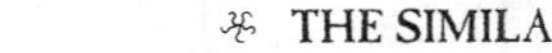

CHAPTER

One

If you're interested in happy stories, trust me when I say that you'd be far better off reading something else. You'd no doubt prefer one of those *Harry Potter* books, or *Teen People*, or even the back of a package of Lunchables. Because the book you're about to read is not happy at all. And that's fine — but the bigger problem is that it is also not innovative, clever or particularly entertaining. In fact, it's filled with one unfortunate, repetitive, derivative, tedious, repetitive twist of fate after another. Furthermore, even if you feel the need to read more than just one of these paper-thin episodes, you'd do just as well by reading the first 10 pages and last 10 pages

of the book. The rest is really just an appalling amount of filler. So, why not stop now and find something less aggravating to busy yourself with — it won't be hard to do.

You're still reading, aren't you? Because you're ten books in and you figure that eventually *something* is bound to happen, right? Ha ha! I have you exactly where I want you! *The banana pudding fell sideways into the giraffe's lap*. You read that too, didn't you? Keep reading, it's bound to pay off in a big way real soon! Sucker!

By now, you know all about the Baudelaires — there's the eldest, Violet, who is always inventing things; then there's Klaus, the middle child, who is constantly reading things; and, of course, there's Sunny, the baby, who is always biting things. This is not a summary — this is actually the full extent of the character development after 10 novels' worth of stories. You're up to speed!

Often, while laying awake at night, alone and scared, I wish I had never begun my investigation of the Baudelaires — an endeavor that has ruined my life, forcing me to write, essentially, the same story nearly a dozen times. Of course, when I lie awake at night, it is in my mansion, atop my diamond-filled mattress, and I drift into sleep as soon as I think about how this drivel has made me a millionaire many, many times over — so I won't linger on that particular problem for too long — and neither should you.

At this point in the Baudelaires' truly unfortunate lives, they were in a situation exactly like what they had experienced countless times before. Mr. Poe was about to leave them with a new guardian.

The Baudelaires, of course, were nervous about meeting this distant relative/friend of the family/friend of a friend of a family/disinterested third party (depending on what's easiest for the story — it doesn't much matter, they won't be sticking around long). Actually, "nervous" was a remarkably well-adjusted state of mind for them to be in — considering that their parents had burned to death, they themselves had nearly been murdered on countless occasions, and no one seemed too bothered by the pattern. Still, they had butterflies in their stomachs just the same.

"Who will we be living with?" Violet asked.

"Oh, it's a zany, inept individual who has an odd fear or obsession that you'll have to abide by, making it impossible to solve your parents' murder or to keep Count Olaf from reentering your lives," Mr. Poe gruffly explained, pausing to cough into his handkerchief.

"You mean like our Aunt Josephine, who wouldn't let us use the stove for any reason?" Klaus asked, rolling his eyes.

"Or 'Sir' at the mill, who wouldn't let us say a word in his presence?" Violet asked.

"Or Jerome Squalor, who refused to disagree with anything his evil, shallow wife said?" Klaus asked.

"Well, our last guardian was absurdly cruel and inept," Violet pointed out, "so I guess that means this guardian will be *good-natured* and inept."

"Crackers!" Sunny said, which probably meant something like, "That's the pattern!"

Sunny, though quite young and capable of only gibberish, was absolutely correct — the characters were all pretty much amorphous — a fancy word in this case meaning "another example of unimaginative, half-witted character development on the writer's part."

"Why can't we live with Justice Strauss, the one person who's been nice to us and believed us about Count Olaf?" Klaus asked.

"You can only be adopted by a relative — that is the rule," Mr. Poe wheezed, a thick strand of phlegm dangling from the corner of his mouth to his ever-present handkerchief.

"But," Violet added, "what about the Squalors — they were just family friends?"

"Well…" Mr. Poe began.

"Or that vile village?" Klaus asked, "We weren't related to any of those people!"

"Same goes for that miserable mill," Violet noted.

"Korn!" Sunny said, by which she probably meant, "And what about when Count Olaf nearly adopted us while he was posing as a female secretary, even though 'she' wasn't related to us at all…"

"Please don't talk to me while I'm driving," Mr. Poe said, conveniently cutting off the children as so many other adults had done when they were asking perfectly reasonable questions. But it was just as well, since Mr. Poe and the children had arrived at their destination — the home of the Baudelaires' new guardian.

CHAPTER Three

"*Hello*," said the kindly figure who rushed up to greet them, "I'm Jesse Happy, your new guardian. I just want you to know that I believe you about Count Olaf — and I swear I'll do everything in my power to keep him from ever coming near you again. We're going to have so much fun together, children! We're going to go on picnics and see movies and laugh at funny jokes..."

The Baudelaires felt that at last they had found a home — and with it, a guardian with whom they could find safety and happiness. But, as I've gone nearly four pages without stating, this is not a happy story — and the Baudelaires' happiness, no matter how great, was to be ending very soon.

For just as Jesse was about to make colorful balloon animals for the children, he was crushed beneath the wheels of a car — meeting the predictably gruesome fate of every adult who is kind to the Baudelaires.

"Well," Mr. Poe said, "that's another guardian you've managed to louse up. Tell you what, though, we'll see if this reckless driver is interested in caring for a few wayward orphans."

"I sure *would* be!" was the immediate reply from the unusual man who stepped out of the car, deliberately crushing the windpipe of a still-squirming Jesse in the process.

He wore a headband low over his eyebrows and a giant gaudy anklet that was big enough to hide an incriminating ankle tattoo. He also wore a white t-shirt that had big black letters that read, "I am NOT Count Olaf."

"Allow me to introduce myself," he said, scraping bits of hair and skin off of his fender and pausing only to pry an ear from his hood ornament, "I'm Count Falo."

The Baudelaires, of course, saw past his lame disguise and painfully phony name and realized that, just like clockwork, their old nemesis Count Olaf had reared his ugly head yet again.

"Mr. Poe," Klaus screamed in outrage and surprise, "that is not 'Count Falo' — it is none other than Count Olaf!"

"Nonsense," Mr. Poe exclaimed, "he is wearing a shirt that clearly states he is NOT Count Olaf! He wouldn't be allowed to wear such a garment if it weren't true."

Of course, everyone knows that that is not the case. Obviously, just because something is written on a t-shirt, that does not make it fact. A person wearing a t-shirt that says "Girls Gone Wild!" does not necessarily work for that company — even if he *does* have a camera and swears that he'll make you a star. Everybody knows this — except perhaps for my poor, departed, flash-happy paramour, Beatrice. And, unfortunately for the Baudelaires, Mr. Poe was equally obtuse — a word which here means "super stupid."

But I'm getting off on a tangent — a word that here means, "a bit of unrelated nonsense used to stretch out a flimsy story." So, Count Olaf had already re-emerged — and the Baudelaires could immediately see through his disguise, but would be unable to convince Mr. Poe — or anyone else — until the end of the story. Meaning that there were now 100 mind-numbing pages before every other dense character realized what you, young reader, deduced on page 21. Enjoy!

"Seriously, Mr. Poe," Violet said, "he's Count Olaf...come

on…don't be such a jackass about this!"

"Rozzer!" Sunny said, which probably meant something along the lines of, "For Christ's sake! How many times do we have to go through this exact same scenario! Even *I'm* starting to get tired of this — and I have no short-term memory whatsoever!"

Turning to face the Baudelaires once more, Mr. Poe said, "Now calm down children — the only other time I've seen you this worked up was right before all those times when I left you in the custody of someone who turned out to be Count Olaf!"

"You'll have to forgive the children, Count Falo — they're just upset because Count Olaf always turns up and tries to murder them and every adult they get close to. You know how cranky and suspicious children can get when they have the constant threat of homicide hanging over their heads!"

"It's no problem at all," "Count Falo" said with a smile, "I've tried to kill them so many times, I've nearly lost count!"

"Are you even listening to what he's saying right now?!?" Violet screamed.

"Violet," Mr. Poe said, turning away from "Count Falo" to address the eldest Baudelaire, "it's not polite to yell — and please stop kicking me in the groin while you're at it!"

As Mr. Poe was scolding Violet, behind him, "Count Falo" was holding Sunny by her ankles and using her to beat Klaus about the face and neck, bloodying both in the process.

"But Mr. Poe, if you'll just turn your head 90 degrees, you'll see that phony 'Count Falo' is abusing both my brother and sister right this very minute!"

"Violet, please, it's not polite for children to ask adults to turn their heads. And Klaus, stop that screaming and begging for mercy! Why can't you children behave yourselves?!?"

Oftentimes, adults will not believe children. Maybe it's because they're smaller and sometimes prone to exaggeration. Or maybe it's because adults don't like to think that children know more than they do about certain things. Or, most often, an adult won't listen to a child simply because stubborn adults are an excellent cover for sloppy, inconsistent writers.

"Oh, heavens!" Mr. Poe exclaimed, finally looking at Klaus and Sunny, just after Count Falo had finally grown tired of beating them up and had kicked Sunny, soft-spot-first, directly into Klaus' solar plexus. "Your brother and sister have somehow managed to get blood all over their clothes and faces! You children are behaving most peculiarly today!"

"Yes, but…" Klaus said woozily, feeling several broken ribs floating around his midsection.

"No 'buts,'" Mr. Poe said, "I'm late for a very important appointment. You're in excellent hands — Count Falo is practically family. Good day."

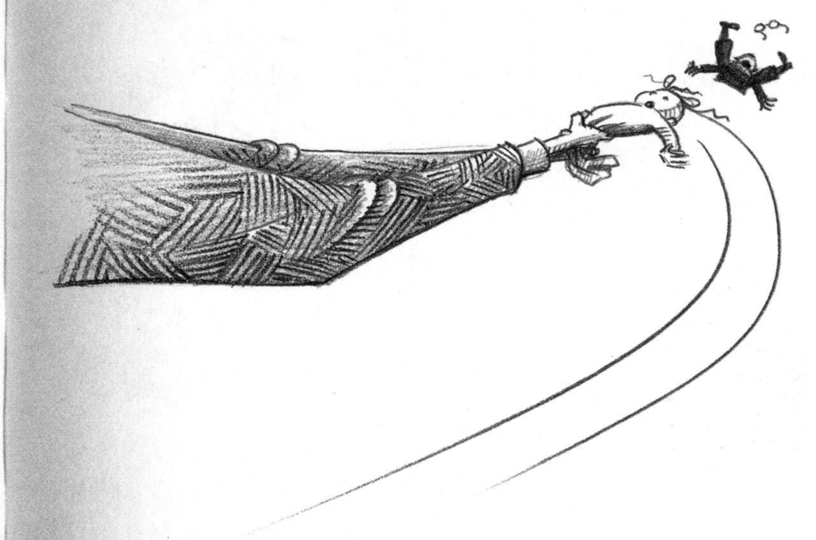

CHAPTER Eight

"*What* I don't understand," Violet said, turning to her brother, "is how Count Olaf's plan even makes any sense now. Ever since he first tried to steal our inheritance, he's definitely not included in our parents' will — and simply being related to us certainly doesn't entitle him to anything. Plus, after all the terrible, illegal things that he's done, he's a wanted criminal. There's no way that a man wanted for several murders would be awarded any part of our fortune."

"That's troubled me too," said Klaus.

"Klaus," Violet asked suddenly, "do you remember that time when we were all going to go on a picnic, but it ended up raining?"

"Yes," Klaus said, wistfully remembering one of the many happy days he shared with his family before his parents were killed in that horrible fire and the Baudelaires were forced to endure one miserable experience after another. "It was far too stormy to go outside, but we had a picnic right on the living room rug."

"Dropsy!" Sunny chirped in — which meant something along the lines of, "Yes, I too remember all the fun we used to have with our parents! Good times!"

As the Baudelaires lay in their beds, they thought of their parents futilely clawing the walls and screaming in agony as the flames melted the flesh right off their charred bones.

"Oh well, enough reminiscing. It's silly to dwell on the past," Violet concluded, ending this adventure's obligatory recollection of their parents.

CHAPTER Ten

"*We're* trapped!" Klaus shouted.

"I don't know how we'll ever get out of this spot!" Violet exclaimed.

The spot she was speaking of, of course, was page 121 — roughly the same spot where the Baudelaires get "hopelessly" trapped in every single one of their adventures.

"Unless…" Klaus said, indicating a breakthrough that readers are not supposed to be able to predict.

"I seem to remember reading a book on 'convenient plot solutions.' I think that bit of information I've recalled, combined with Sunny biting something into pieces with her two sharp teeth and you inventing something clever at the last minute, should be just what we need to get out of this jam and make one last, uneventful attempt to capture Count Olaf. Good thing I read that book!"

And without a trace of familiarity for the situation, Violet took a ribbon out of her pocket and tied her hair up, as she always did when she needed to invent something that would miraculously save them.

"What are you inventing, Violet?" Klaus asked, purely for tradition's sake.

"Snide!" Sunny said, which meant something along the line of, "She's inventing a 'plot device.' She's going to take the few 'random,' seemingly unrelated objects in her direct vicinity and create an invention at the very last second that perfectly suits the obstacle at hand! Stuck in a runaway elevator? She'll invent an 'elevator-stopper'! About to be trampled by rampaging elephants? She'll invent an 'elephant-disperser'! God! This nonsense makes *MacGyver* look Shakespearean!"

Within a few minutes, Violet had taken two lollipops, the "XYZ" volume of the 1977 World Book and an old shower cap and made an invention that perfectly solved their conundrum — a word that in this case means "imbroglio."

If this were a happy story, it would have a happy ending — and the villain would be captured, while the heroes would be left cheerful, and perhaps enjoying a chocolate sundae (unless they were lactose intolerant, in which case, a non-dairy treat could be easily substituted).

And if you're still expecting a happy ending, you're clearly some sort of moron — although it HAS been nearly four pages since I last stressed that this is NOT a traditional happy story.

Anyway, as those of you who read the previous sentence may remember, this story does NOT have a happy ending. It will, however, have an abrupt, unsatisfactory and well-worn ending. Happy endings are unrealistic and boring and predictable. In contrast, unhappy endings are dark and edgy and unexpected! Even with plenty of previous warnings. In book after book. After book.

CHAPTER Twelve

"*Count* Olaf is getting away!" Violet said.

"*We'll* have to stop him then!" the orphans shouted, somehow conveniently finding the courage to face Count Olaf that had eluded them for the previous 138 pages.

"Oh, heavens no!" Mr. Poe said, hacking into a brown, dripping handkerchief. "I can't allow you to be endangered by pursuing that criminal. I am charged with your well-being. Let the police apprehend him…"

"But Count Olaf is right *there*!" Klaus said.

"He's ordering a drink at that coffee shop!" Violet yelled. "Now he's going into the theater to watch *The Return of the King* — he'll be there for the next three and a half hours!"

"No, no," Mr. Poe said, as he expelled a large bloody mass into his handkerchief, "better that we stay put. The police will handle it — we'll give them a call first thing tomorrow."

"The police are useless idiots!" Klaus screamed. "If they really want to catch Count Olaf, why don't they just stay with us and wait for Olaf to turn up and harass us like he does every single freakin' time!?!"

"Seriously," Violet shouted, "what kind of cops can't find a lanky, sinister man accompanied by a half-dozen cohorts who have hook-hands, incredibly pale skin and other immediately identifiable and freakish traits?!? These aren't people who just blend into a crowd!"

"Poiuyt!" Sunny said, sinking both of her large pointy teeth directly into Mr. Poe's Achilles' tendon. If Mr. Poe weren't in such pain, he might have realized that what she said meant something like, "And if you're so freakin' concerned with our safety, why do you put us with one horrible, unfit guardian after another?!?"

CHAPTER Thirteen

"*If* only we could find a way to figure out what our friends, the Quagmire triplets, discovered about our problems," Violet said, frustrated. "What's V.F.D. stand for? And why was there a secret passageway underneath our old, burned home? And is one of our parents still alive?

"Oh, it's no use," she said, letting her hair fall across her face and giving up on the thought process, "we could never duplicate their research! We're only the three smartest grade-schoolers in the world — we could never find the same facts about our own family that two total strangers were able to discover after a *whole afternoon* in the library!"

"Well, it's not all bad," Klaus said, finding the same bright side that the orphans always found after another nearly-deadly and pointless adventure. "We're still together, and we did manage to defeat Count Olaf once again!"

"Potrzebie!" Sunny shrieked — which in this case meant something along the lines of, "and we're also no further along in this story than when we *started*, morons!"

At this point, I'll simply end the story and attempt to make up for another flat and disappointing conclusion by going directly to my note to the editor, vaguely hinting at the possibility of plot development in the next unfulfilling and formulaic installment. I'd explain what "formulaic" means — but I've already met my word count. See you next time, suckers!

To My Kind Editor,

I am writing to you from the humongous whirlpool bathtub of my Italian penthouse. Oh...that is to say I'm writing to you from...oh, let's say, "The Dangerous Dam"...or "The Treacherous Trolley," or "The Hectic Halfway-House." Or whatever – just pick something vaguely sinister and alliterative and I'll plug it into the standard template.

Anyway, for the sake of this letter, let's say that I'm visiting the home of the Baudelaires' "mean and idiosyncratic guardian" and I'm looking for anything that would shed some light on the time that the Baudelaires spent there.

Please go to Eli's Bagels on Route 34 at 3 P.M. next Wednesday and order a pumpernickel bagel with vegetable cream cheese. It will not help you at all in piecing together this story, but it's delicious, and it's well worth the effort. Afterwards, visit the nearby Strathmore Cinema and buy a children's ticket to Gigli. Sit in the first seat on your right – beneath it, you will find an envelope. I guarantee you will have plenty of privacy to read its contents. Inside, you will find my notes, as well as a tooth from the silent sloth, a coaster from the Tavern on the Scream Bar & Grill and a sketch of Carmen Electra that I'm particularly proud of. On second thought, I'll just send a messenger over with it after I'm done with this afternoon's deep tissue massage. Ciao!

Remember, you are my only hope to keep this sweet, sweet money-maker going by publishing a yearly edition of this endless saga. Don't screw it up for both of us.

With all due respect,

~~Daniel Handler~~ Lemony Snicket

Lemony Snicket

WRITER AND ARTIST: ANTONIO PROHIAS COLORIST: CARRIE STRACHAN

MAD PRESENTS The Least Pop

ular Wii Games

WRITER: TOM SILVESTRO ARTIST: KEVIN POPE

Summer means just one thing! Complete, constant freedom… for about a day or so. Then, if you want to actually do anything, you'll need a job to pay for it! But just because you've got to work, that doesn't mean you have to take the first job that comes along! Before you agree to put on that hairnet and plastic smock, here are some…

THINGS TO CONSIDER BEFOR…

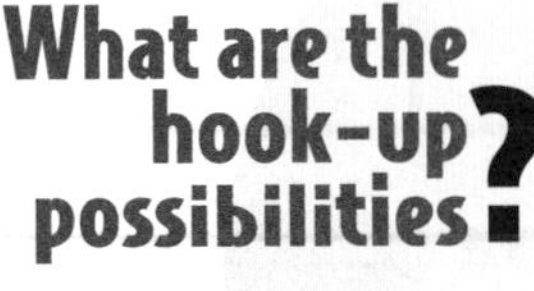

Are there any, um, inmates or whatever, that are under, like, thirty? Or even forty?

How lame are the uniforms?

Will you be able to get there and back?

Are the fringe benefits cool or sucky?

WRITER AND ARTIST: TERESA BURNS PARKHURST

CCEPTING A SUMMER JOB

What's the humiliation factor?

Abby Smeadnoff? I haven't seen you since A.P. Physics! What have you been up to?

Will there be a lingering smell?

I'm breaking up with you because you stink of Bloomin' Onion every second.

Do you get to operate cool machines?

Sorry, Mr. Tibbutts, I didn't mean to give you another 'Nam freak-out...I was just seeing how this baby handles a cup of pennies.

Would you be happier just being broke?

So, if it's a loosey bowel, Marsha needs a Freshens wipe, but if she's straining to go, you might have to coax her digitally – oh, and she loves to humpy wrestle!

Will you end up with a good reference?

Well, Josh, I wasn't able to contact a "Mr. Smith"...apparently "Lawnmower Dudes" is no longer in business and he won't be up for parole for another six months.
Well, there was that old lady whose car I washed...oh wait – she's dead...

TALES FROM THE DUCK SIDE DEPT.

THE MEATY MERMAID MENACE

ARTIST AND WRITER: DUCK EDWING

SERGE-IN GENERAL DEPT.

SERGIO ARAGONES PRESENTS A MAD LOOK

WRITER AND ARTIST: SERGIO ARAGONES

macy's

NEWS
4

PIZZA

PIZZA

PIZZA

TOC
THUND
TUN

RIP
JOE

RIP
JOE

PIZZA

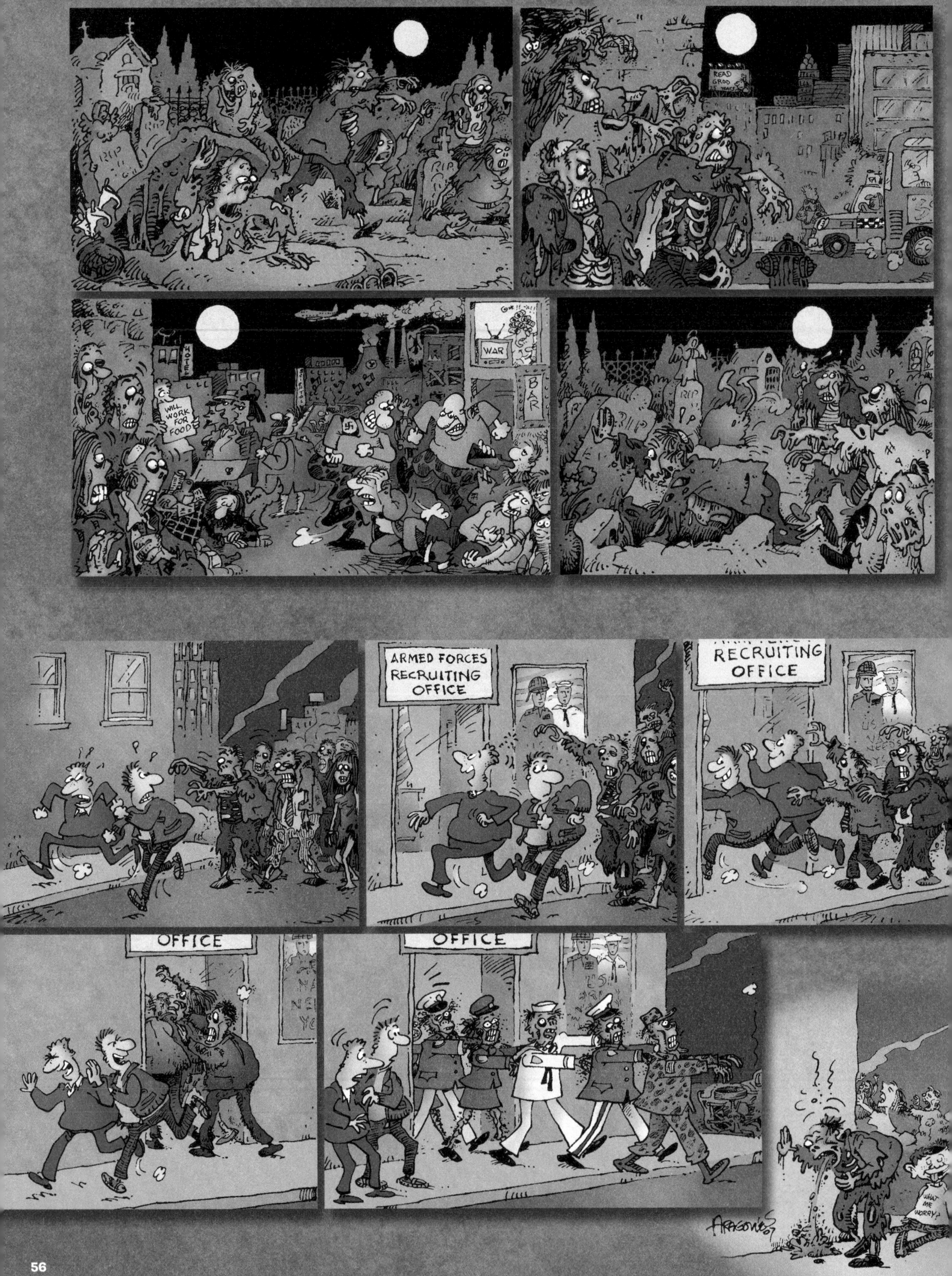

READ GROO
HOTEL
WILL WORK FOR FOOD
WAR
BAR
ARMED FORCES RECRUITING OFFICE
RECRUITING OFFICE
OFFICE
OFFICE
WHAT ME WORRY?
ARAGONÉS

One Fine Day in the Operating Room

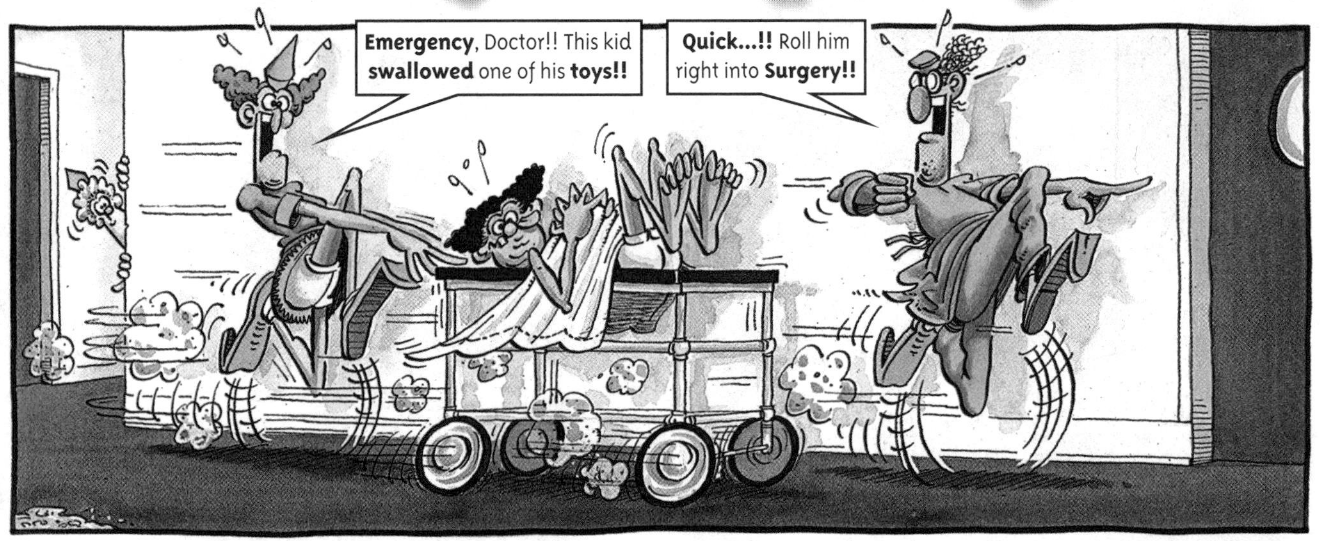

WRITER: DON EDWING ARTIST: DON MARTIN

BEATING A DEAD NORSE DEPT.

MAD'S THOR-OUGHLY STUPID THOR OUTTAKES

600 bucks on StubHub and I can't even see Bono!
He says he has no health insurance! GET HIM OUT OF HERE!!!

If I call it
"Bat-arang,"
aybe it'll make
this movie
watchable.

What's that, abs? You sense danger lurking about?

You go in for a routine check-up, and BAM! — strapped down like Hannibal Lecter! Thanks, ObamaCare!

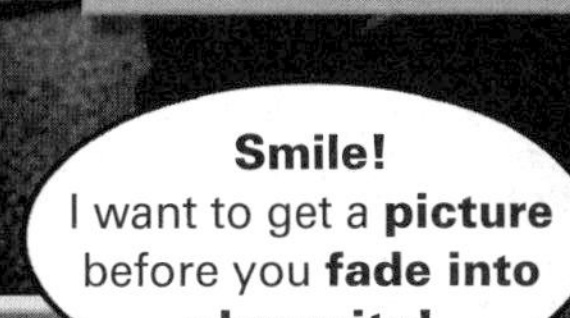
Smile! I want to get a picture before you fade into obscurity!

And together, we WILL remodel the second bathroom!!!

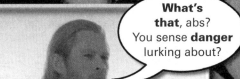

The Castaway

WRITER: AL JAFFEE ARTIST: PAUL COKER

Take One
Free
We'll Make
Up For It
Somewhere Else

www.clunkermagazine.con

Your Totaled Transportation Tabloid
Including: New Vehicles, Used Vehicles, and *Really* Used Vehicles

Vol. XXI Issue 05

92 DODGE CRAPAVAN 1-wheel drive, turbo-charged price tag, w/sturdy, stainless steel airbag. Owner's manual in braille. $37,000. PRIVATE PARTY, 121-2405

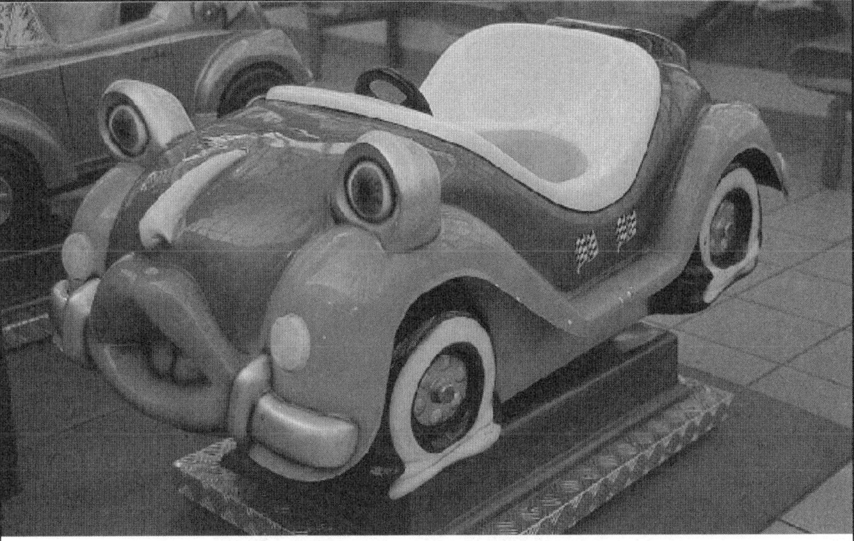

82 LINCOLN CLOWN CAR
External combustion engine, tubeless ashtray, aquarium windows, trampoline roof, convex rearview mirrors like at carnival fun houses. $17,505. WRECKY'S CARZ, 161-5383

93 WHITE FORD BRONCO Xlnt cond., $17,000 ($25,000 for idiots who make lame, predictable references to O.J.). BY OWNER, 181-8900

94 CHEVY LUNATIC Chrome wheels, traction ctrl. & little purple man in glove compartment revealing secrets of Roswell. $16,354. PRIVATE PARTY, 197-3678

91 INFINNITY Intentionally misspelled name, Formica dash, EZ-rip faux leather seats, invisible multi-disc CD player. $14,000. THE CAR DITCH, 160-2949

95 FORD PHELGM 1 cyl., coal-powered, solid gold splash guards. Horn plays first eight notes of "A Hundred Bottles Of Beer On The Wall." $15,600. AUTO DUMP, 160-9483

Unless otherwise specified, price(s) include(s) all Cost(s) to be paid by consumer(s) except for license(s), tax(es), back parking ticket(s), upholstery cleaning(s) and many other things you'll find out as you go along.

To Place Your Photo Ad
1-800-BAD-PIX

Targeting Drivers Who Don't Care What Others Think About Them

That Number Again
1-800-BAD-PIX

97 TOYOTA MOSQUITO
Comes w/mysterious stains, wood paneling one one side, in-dash steering wheel. Rear-seat soda dispenser! $14,000. PRIVATE PARTY, 191-9001

99 HONDA ACCORDION
Includes pre-nicked windshield and factory installed spice rack. Perfect 2nd car if you only use the 1st one. $18,750. DOODLE MOTORS, 141-7888

86 FORD INSIPID
Like new, only not. Speedometer in Roman numerals, mini jaws-of-life in glove compartment, body in trunk. $4450. BY OWNER, 500-0001.

65 MUSTANG
Electric pink collector's classic with AM/FM stereo, CD changer and leather bucket seats would be really nice, but all I have is this 89 Sentra. $199. PRIVATE PARTY, 130-5332

86 CADILLAC BROUGHAM
Sick purple, Y2K compliant cup-holder. Must sell, or my bookie will send his goons out to break my legs. $6500 PLEEEZE! BY OWNER, 151-2649

95 VW BURRITO
Obnoxious semi-gloss ext., special hidden compartment for hiding open bottles of syrup, illegal aliens, etc. $12,500. PRIVATE PARTY, 171-7171

BAD CREDIT?
NO CREDIT?
WOW, YOU MUST BE A REAL LOSER!

CRAZY HOWIE'S AUTO ASYLUM 1-900-HEAP

Se Habla Your Cash

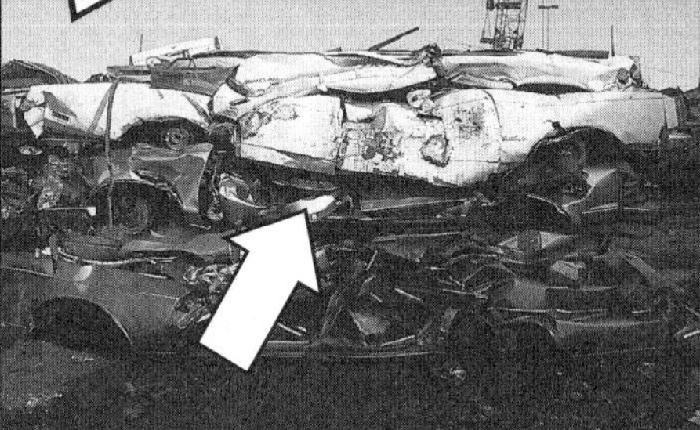

97 ELECTRIC CAR
Runs great on 10,000 AA batteries (not incl). Buy now, before the federal gov't sells out to big oil and puts us all in gulags. $12,500.

96 MITSUBISHI SUSHI
Comes with 7G blrp and 364 qltv. dual glp. New 1876+ krn. w/28W clg. and extra fsh. Auto 6 cc ft base wls and dim vims. Optional veckers. $20,000.

95 NISSAN 200SX
Seeks romantic encounter with other 200SX Enjoys trips through countryside, car washes wax jobs, and candlelight oil changes.

91 DODGE AFFRONT
1 spd. 100% dolphin skin int, semi-translucent windows. Handles okay considering it's never been inspected. $5600.

92 CHEVY WIDOWMAKER
Fully loaded w/reel-to-reel, turbo-charged smog spewer, stolen license plates and complimentary half-eaten bag of Fritos in back seat. Was $18,750, now $18,449.

63 NASH METRO
900,000+ miles, runs like 600,000. Origina tires. 1984 Mondale for President bumper stk (non-removable). $24,300.

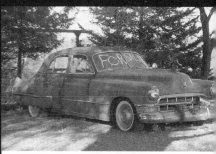

GOVERNMENT-SEIZED VEHICLE AUCTION!

U.S. Government is auctioning vehicles seized in drug raids, jaywalking busts or just when they felt like hassling someone. With luck, you'll find something in the trunk they missed when they searched it!

MODEL	SOLD FOR	BLUE BOOK	SAVINGS
95 FORD SIESTA	$10,000	$10,000	$2500
94 HOT WHEELS BENTLEY	$15.00	NONE	$15.00
92 MAZDA MALARIA	$7,000	$6,000	-$1,000
99 VW MILLENNIUM BUG	$2,000	$2,000	$0.00
63 FORD CLOWNBIRD	$5,500	$10,000	-$3,000
93 TOYOTA RELICA	N/A	N/A	$2,000
94 HONDA DISCORD	$7,500	$6,000	$2,500
97-98 JAGUAR SEASON TICKETS	$1,750	-$2,000	$4,000
89 FORD MODELING AGENCY	$4,500	$3,5000	N/A
79 NASA MOON BUGGY	$2,000	$2,000	$0.00
95 CHEVY LUPICA	$5,500	$10,000	-$3,000
96 HONDA ODDITY	N/A	N/A	$2,000
93 OLDS GUTLESS	$7,500	$6,000	$2,500
96 HYUNDAI ACCIDENT	$1,750	-$2,000	$4,000
96 NISSAN ULTERIOR	$4,500	$3,500	N/A
93 DODGE PRAM	$0.00	$4.95	$1,700
92 CADILLAC EVILLE	43¢	89¢	46¢
92 TOYOTA SCAMRY	$9,000	$14,000	$5,000
95 MITSUBISHI RELAPSE	$7,000	$6,000	-$1,000
92 GEO SCHISM	$3,000	$4,450	$2,000
94 DODGE ENTRAPPED	$2,000	$2,000	$0.00
96 KIA SARCOMA	$5,500	$10,000	-$3,000
97 TOYOTA CELIBATE	$7,500	$6,000	$2,500
94 MAZDA PROTOZOAN	$1,750	-$2,000	$4,000
95 FORD DETOUR	$4,500	$3,5000	N/A
94 CHEVY IMPALER	$2,000	$2,000	$0.00
92 TOYOTA PASSÉ	$5,500	$10,000	-$3,000
95 PONTIAC BONEMEAL	N/A	N/A	$2,000
72 CADILLAC ELDORKO	$7,500	$6,000	$2,500
96 DODGE GRIPER	$1,750	-$2,000	$4,000
90 CHEVY DECEASE	$4,500	$3,500	N/A
95 VW FACADE	$3,000	$2,999	$1.00
97 TOYOTA GLAUCOMA	$0.00	$4.95	$1,700
91 ALFRED E. ROMEO	43c	89c	46c
68 PONTIAC TORQUEMADA	$7,000	$6,000	-$1,000
88 TOYOTA CORRODED	$2,000	$2,000	$0.00
93 SLAAB 900S	$5,500	$10,000	-3,000
93 CHEVY ASTROS FAN	N/A	N/A	$2,000
97 PONTIAC SUNSTROKE	$6,500	$2,000	$2,000
96 MERCURY MISTAKE	$7,500	$6,000	$2,500
90 IZUZU NOPULSE	$1,750	-$2,000	$4,000
93 HYUNDAI CILANTRO	$4,500	$3,500	N/A
86 HONDA DELUDE	$3,000	$2,999	$1.00
91 CHEVY LUSITANIA	$0.00	$4.95	$1,700
90 CHRYSLER IMPEACHABLE	$-500	$2,750	$-3,250
92 PONTIAC FIASCO	43¢	89¢	46¢
91 DODGE CAROM VAN	$9,000	$14,000	$5,000

Terms: Payment in full within 15 minutes of sale.

BIG ED'S USED CARS & PETS

170-2186

This offer is not being made by any U.S. government agency, but we sure try to make it look that way.

TELL THEM YOU SAW IT IN THE JALOPY SHOPPER

(So they'll think the smeared ink and dark, blurry photos were only in *their* copy!)

96 CHRYSLER MARQUI DeSADE
3 1/2 door, diesel eng., radio only picks up Spanish gospel stations. Special $1,000 extra charge for women buyers. $29,999. ACME CAR DITCH, 120-3984

1993 WINNEBAGO DELUX
Kitchenette, den w/fireplace, shower, nursery, weight rm, walk-in closet, baseball diamond, lobby, veterinary clinic, horseback trails. $34,400. JIM'S RV & UNICYCLE WORLD, 190-3440

74 SNOWMOBILE
Haunted by ghost of former owner who ran it off cliff. Does not run well in cold weather. $8,000. PRIVATE PARTY, 131-8275

96 FORD POLYP
AM/FM mono, plush leather ext. Must have 5 yrs. Exp., type 90 wpm, 2 yrs of college. $44,003. BY OWNER, 180-5902

94 SUBPARU
Woodgrain chassis, cruise control stuck on 110 mph. Must repair to appreciate. $13,000. PRIVATE PARTY, 140-2383

98 TOYZUKI WREC-4
Radar detects ice cream trucks within 5 miles, wheels on hood for when it tips over. $17,440. BY OWNER, 171-6450.

91 LUNCHWAGON
Near-xlnt cond., except for smell of stale salami, various bullet holes & Freon leaks. $34,127. TRUCK DORKS, 150-8554

33 BENTLEY
Looks exactly like a Volkswagen bug. Must be seen to almost believe. $150,000. PRIVATE PARTY, 161-5898

No need to mention that you saw it in the JALOPY SHOPPER

THE DWAYNE CHRONICLES

WRITER AND ARTIST: ERIC SCOTT

THE BELCHING DRAGON

CHINESE FOOD to EAT IN or TAKE OUT

NOODLES

- 穷水尽 *Cellophane Noodles with Styrofoam Peanuts....5.50
- 烟瘴气 Some Glum Noodles....8.25
- 冰天地 No Fun Noodles....4.75
- 雨天 Wacky Water Noodles in Pool of Garlic Sauce....5.25

POULTRY

- 平浪 *Lemon Pledge Chicken....6.25
- 冰天 Mocked Duck....7.25
- 雨天青 Goofy Grinning Chicken....6.75
- *Tongue Licked Duck....7.50
- 烟 *Sesame Street Duck....11.75

SEAFOOD & PORK

- 风平浪 Aromatic Octopus On Wheels....10.50
- 穷 *Flounder with Water Pistol....8.95
- 天 New Shoe Pork....6.75
- 烟瘴 Recently Shampooed Pork....6.95

BEEF

- 穷水 Air-Dropped Beef....6.85
- 平浪 *Beef with More Beef....7.75
- 烟瘴气 Beef And Dried Pepper Spilled on Lap....9.25
- 冰天地 *Great Barrier Beef....6.85
- 天 *What's Your Beef....7.25

SOUPS & APPETIZERS

- 雨天 Dropped Egg Soup....1.75
- 穷水尽 *One Ton Soup....1.75
- 天 Hot & Scalding Soup....2.25
- 穷水尽 Ten Ingredients Water....3.25
- 风平浪 *Happy Bacteria Cup....2.50
- 烟瘴 Steam-Cleaned Dumplings....3.95
- 井石 *Burn Your Tongue Platter....8.95

VEGETABLES

- 穷水 *Bean Crud with Special Rotting Fungus....6.25
- 天 *Snow Shovel with Peas....7.75
- 水尽 Green Beans with Black Bean Sauce....4.95
- 平浪 Black Beans with Green Bean Sauce....5.95
- Stir-Crazy Vegetables....4.25
- 雨天 *Baby Corn with Adoption Papers....4.95
- 穷 Vegetables with Tingling Horse Flavor....5.50

DESSERTS

- 尽 Unfortunate Cookies....2.50
- 浪 Sweet Fried Altoids....3.95
- 烟瘴气 Ice Cream with Garlic Sauce....2.75
- 地 *Boneless Pudding....3.50
- 天青 Chicken Almond Ring Ding....3.95

50 lbs. white rice with every order

*May Not Be Edible

Free can of soda with orders over $1,000.00

A MAD FAKEOUT MENU

WRITERS: CHARLIE KADAU AND JOE RAIOLA
ARTIST: GEORGE WOODBRIDGE

THE PROBLEMS WITH HAVING A
SUPERHERO
AS A NEIGHBOR!
HAWKMAN
No matter where I park, that winged fool nails my car every morning!
SPIDER-MAN
My wash! My nice clean wash!
AQUAMAN
Whoops... made a wrong turn again! Hi there, I live next door!
THE HULK
He "Hulks Out" like this every tim his team fumbles

BATMAN
That huge
atmobile is always
blocking our
driveway!
THE THING
It's ball
clobberin' time!
Can you please stop inviting Ben Grimm to our softball games? We're going broke replacing the ball every time he gets up to bat!
WOLVERINE
Darn! His hedges always look better than mine! He's a show-off!
BEN 10
Every Halloween it's the same thing — we get cleaned out of candy when Ben 10 shows up at our house ten times!
WRITER: DUCK EDWING ARTIST: JOHN KERSCHBAUM

A MAD LOOK AT

SEALS WATER-PARK
SEALS WATER-PARK
MANAGER

POOLS
SUPER!
CLAIRE BEAR WATER-PARK
Park
PARKING

TUBES 5⁰⁰

PARKING
B

WATER PARKS

WRITER AND ARTIST: SERGIO ARAGONÉS

BATHROOMS

ONLY

NO

SOAP

ARAGONES 02.

THE WORST PIÑATA DESIGNS EVER!

If you know your history, you know that secret groups have long held sway over the masses of humanity: The Knights of King Solomon's Temple, The Freemasons, The Trilateral Commission, The Council on Foreign Relations, The Vatican, the second Mickey Mouse Club, Yale's Skull & Bones, parking attendants...the list goes on and on. What? "Parking attendants" you're wondering? Yes, parking attendants — those odd strangers we pay to park our cars. Recently, a source wishing to remain unnamed, slipped us the following shocking document. We promised Marty Kleinfelter never to show it to anyone and after reading it, you'll know why...

The Valet Parking Attendant's Secret Oath

I swear my loyalty to the Apollo Parking System Associates as my witnesses to this oath. I promise to fulfill, according to my negative attitude, poor driving skills, and unfortunate lot in life, this pledge and covenant:

I promise that my tie will always be a different shade of black than the oversized jacket I'm wearing.

Furthermore, I swear that the tie will be a poorly-affixed clip-on, leading drivers to the uneasy conclusion that they are about to leave their $40,000 piece of machinery with someone who is unable to operate a real necktie.

I swear that I will motion for the driver to pull up "just a little more" as soon as he puts the vehicle in park and begins to get out.

On my honor, I will never, *ever*, refuse to park a car with a manual transmission, despite my inability to distinguish the difference between a clutch and a trunk release lever.

I will do my best to guarantee that the driver's claim ticket will be left on his dashboard in a place that is irretrievable to all but the tiny, nimble hands of a double-jointed toddler.

I promise that if I do not simply leave the driver's keys in the ignition of his unlocked, unguarded car, I shall do my best to lose them completely.

I resolve to adjust the car's rearview mirror in a manner that makes the driver incapable of readjusting it back to his liking in under 40 minutes or 25 miles. In addition, I resolve to adjust the seat in a manner that leaves the driver completely immobile and unable to even execute a simple K-turn to come back and complain.

Although I will only drive the car for a few hundred feet, I pledge to adjust all of the radio stations to my tastes and leave the radio's volume raised to a level that will distract the driver, as he drives away, from noticing the screeching of the emergency brake, which I've also left on.

I promise to leave my shirt unlaundered and my body unwashed — creating a noxious, lingering odor in the vehicle that will force the driver to travel with his windows rolled down, even in the dead of winter, just to keep his eyes from tearing.

I promise to continually run my hands through my hair and snack on Cheetos during my shift to ensure that the steering wheel is left covered in an oily, orange-colored sheen.

I duly promise that the length of time it takes me to get the driver's key from the mess on the pegboard, remember where I parked his car and then leisurely stroll to get the vehicle will be long enough to either push the driver past the baby sitter's curfew, into the garage's next hourly price range or both.

If the driver has lost his claim ticket, I pledge to tell him that there is nothing I can do, even if I know exactly which car is his. I also swear to call in no fewer than three coworkers to "consult with on policy" — if only to amuse ourselves and draw attention to his stupidity.

Regardless of my ineptitude or incontrovertible evidence of my guilt, I will swear that I wasn't even the one who parked the car and shall treat the garage's "We are not responsible for lost, stolen, or damaged items" sign as my own personal "Get Out of Jail Free" card.

Finally, I swear that no matter how generous a tip the driver places in my hand, I will grunt and act as though he's just handed me a full colostomy bag.

Duly signed this day ____ of __________, 2004 by

____

Notarized by ______________________________

ARTIST: LIZ LOMAX

WRITER: BUTCH D'AMBROSIO

THE PLIÉ'S THE THING DEPT.

As Natalie Portman showed in *Black Swan*, ballet is a grueling activity that destroys your body, wrecks your mind, and makes you stab Winona Ryder in the face. Unfortunately, all this sacrifice yields very little: a few hours each week, prancing 'round a stage in a frilly leotard. So for all you pirouetters, leapers, and face-stabbers out there, we've helpfully discovered ways for you to make your skills worthwhile! All you need to do is apply...

MAD's 11 Little-Known, Practical, Real Life Uses for Ballet

Situation
Attack by mugger

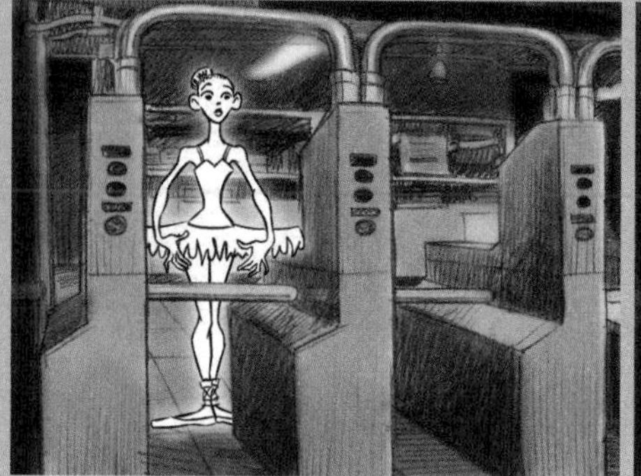

Situation
No money for subway fare

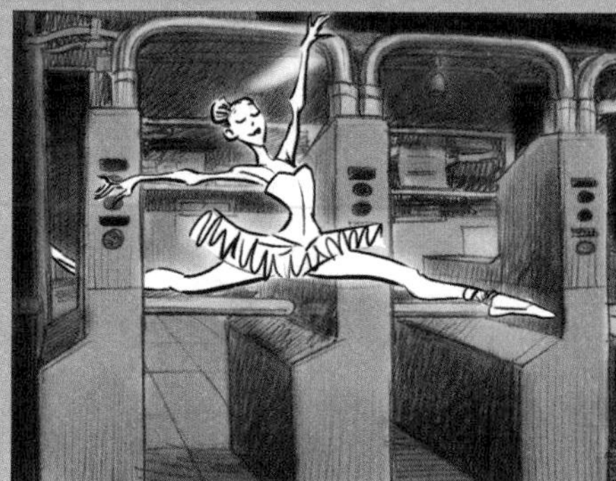

Solution
Grand jeté

Situation
Attack by three muggers

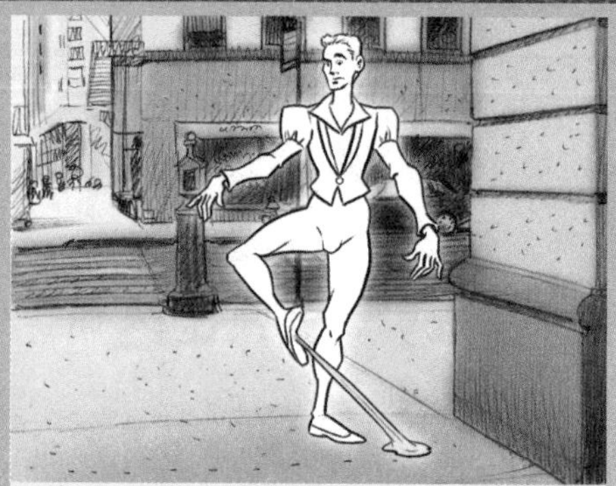

Situation
Gum stuck to bottom of shoe

Solution
Rond de jambe en l'air

Situation
Itchy ankle in crowded eleva

Situation
Annoying door-to-door salesman

Solution
Grand battement en avant

Situation
Creep trying to grab you on subway car

WRITER: MIKE CRAIG ARTIST: JACK SYRACUSE

Solution
Pirouette en dedans

Situation
Squat toilet while on camping trip

Solution
Grand plié

Solution
Second Arabesque

Situation
Sale item on top shelf in supermarket

Solution
Elevé en pointe en premiere with arms en cinquième

Solution
Sur le cou-de-pied

Situation
Dog poop on sidewalk

Solution
Grand pas de chat

Solution
Port de bras in first position (fifth position en avant for Cecchetti students)

Situation
Ate too much at party

Solution
Reverence

THE OLD COWBOY

WRITER: DAVE MANAK ARTIST: AL JAFFEE

PEN AND STINK DEPT.

The COMIC CLUB

JOEY ALISON SAYERS

Lost At See
feggo

The Long and Short of It...

EDMUND BUZZINGTON, YOUR SENTENCE OF DEATH BY ELECTROCUTION WILL NOW BE CARRIED OUT BY THE STATE...

ROB THE EVIL, BACKSTABBING, ROBOT TEMP

WHAT'S GOING ON, MARGARET?

IT'S JIM FROM ACCOUNTING! HE'S... HE'S GOING TO JUMP!

NONE OF US HAVE BEEN ABLE TO TALK HIM OFF THE LEDGE!
LET ME GIVE IT A TRY.

LET'S TALK ABOUT THIS, JIM.

GO AWAY, ROB! MY LIFE IS A WORTHLESS MESS... IT'S TIME TO END IT!

YOU'RE RIGHT, JIM. PERSONALLY, IF I HAD YOUR LIFE, I'D SHOOT MYSELF. BUT, I GUESS JUMPING WORKS TOO.

WELL, I DID MY BEST TO TALK HIM DOWN. DIBS ON HIS STAPLER.

UTTERLY, COMPLETELY, TOTALLY UNDEFEATABLE*... HE'S

FANTABULAMAN

*YES, REALLY.

NO CHALLENGE HAS EVER DEFEATED OUR HERO. BUT WHEN *TIME ITSELF* IS TURNED AGAINST HIM, WILL FANTABULAMAN'S WINNING STREAK AT LAST COME UNDONE?

A VORTEX!
TIME IS LOSING ITS STRUCTURE!!
SOON EVERYTHING WILL BE GONE— EVEN **ME**!

TRAPPED IN AN INCOMPREHENSIBLE VOID, FANTABULAMAN SIZES UP HIS SITUATION.

SOME JERK HAS OBVIOUSLY TRAPPED AND ROTATED A BLACK HOLE TO TAP INTO THE ENERGY NEEDED TO CAUSE QUANTUM FLUCTUATIONS IN GENERAL RELATIVITY, ALLOWING TRAVEL FASTER THAN LIGHT AND THUS TIME REVERSAL, ENABLING HIM TO ERASE THE UNIVERSE BY MESSING WITH THE MOMENT OF CREATION, A.K.A. THE "BIG BANG."

SOMEWHERE/NOWHERE, AT THE EXACT START OF TIME, WE MEET THE EVIL CHRONOMETRIC VILLAIN KNOWN AS THE **CLOCKMASTER**, A.K.A., "SOME JERK"!

NOW THAT I'VE CAPTURED THE BIG BANG, NEITHER FANTABULAMAN NOR THE UNIVERSE WILL EVER EXIST!
NYEH, NYEH, F-MAN!
BIG BANG IN A JAR

BUT THEN—
FANTABULAMAN!? BUT HOW?

BACK-UP FILE.
"BACK-UP FILE"?

YEP. I BACK UP THE UNIVERSE ON MY EXTERNAL HARD DRIVE EVERY NIGHT... JUST IN CASE.
"EVERY NIGHT"? BUT I WASN'T EVEN *HERE* LAST NI—

EXACTLY.
NEXT:
ALIEN INVASION!!

TED RALL

VICTORY ROLL!

WHEATIES

IT ONLY HURTS WHEN I LAUGH

HEY, I WANNA SIGN UP FOR FOOTBALL! I'M READY TO START HITTING THINGS!
FOOTBALL'S MORE THAN JUST HITTING THINGS YOU KNOW.
IT REQUIRES FINESSE.... DEXTERITY!
FOOTBALL

NO IT DOESN'T.
YOU GOTTA BE BUILT LIKE A BRICK WALL, BUT YOU ALSO GOTTA SOAR LIKE AN EAGLE.

SCREW YOUR EAGLE, MAN. AN OFFENSIVE TACKLER JUST NEEDS TO HIT.
OH REALLY? AND YOU THINK YOUR OATMEAL BRAIN KNOWS EVERYTHING ABOUT FOOTBALL?

THEN YOU TELL ME WHAT ELSE THERE IS.
WHAT IS FOOTBALL WITHOUT POETRY, FOR INSTANCE?

THE QUARTERBACK WILL MAKE THE THROW, UP THROUGH THE BLUE THE BALL DOES GO, OR ON FOURTH DOWN UPON THE TOE, HE LETS—

WHAM!

THANKS FOR COVERING BOTH OUR TABLES WHILE I GOT A SODA, RICHIE.
I THINK... I GOT... YOU A... NEW RECRUIT...
FOOTBALL
POETRY CLUB

WRITER AND ARTIST: ANTONIO PROHIAS COLORIST: CARRIE STRACHAN

WEARY OF RELATIVITY DEPT.

As Albert Einstein explained, Time is relative. Which means that, someti Time passes faster or slower than other times. You find that hard to beli

TIME DRAGS..

TIME DRAGS...

...when you're waiting your turn on the roller coaster.

TIME FLIES...

...when you're on the ride.

TIME DRAGS...

...when you're waiting for your Mother in the Hat Department.

TIME DRAGS...

...when your football team is winning by only 2 points.

TIME FLIES...

...when your football team is losing by only 2 points.

TIME DRAGS...

...between being a child... and becoming a young adult.

TIME DRAGS...

...till her parents go out.

TIME FLIES...

...before they come back.

TIME DRAGS...

...between paychecks.

ll, notice how fast Time goes when you're enjoying yourself, as compared to w slow it passes when you're reading a dull article like this one, called . . .

WRITER: STAN HART
ARTIST: JACK RICKARD
COLORIST: CARRIE STRACHAN

TIME FLIES...

ME FLIES...

hen your Mother is waiting
you in the Toy Department.

TIME DRAGS...

...waiting for Xmas morning,
so you can open your presents.

TIME FLIES...

...before they're all broken.

ME FLIES...

tween being a young adult
d becoming an old adult.

TIME DRAGS...

...waiting for someone to
get out of the bathroom.

TIME FLIES...

...before someone wants you
to get out of the bathroom.

ME FLIES...

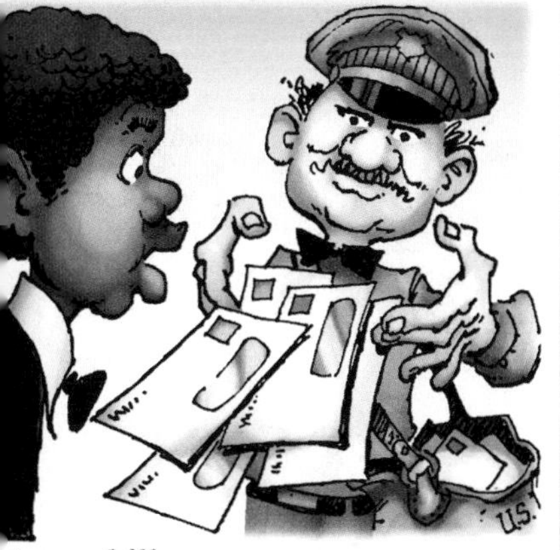

tween bills.

TIME FLIES...

...between Dentist appointments.

TIME DRAGS...

...when he's drilling your tooth.

THE MAG

CIAN

WRITER AND ARTIST:
DON MARTIN

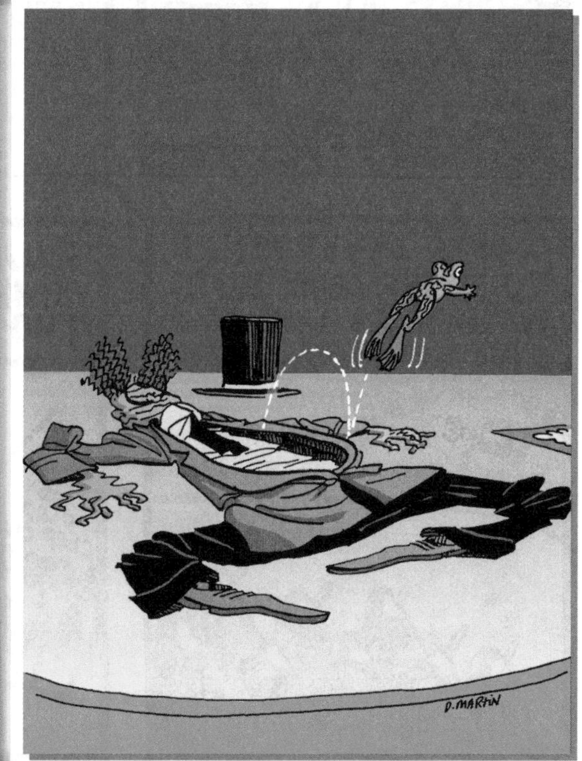

MOCK OF THE PENGUINS

I SEEN THAT MOVIE 'BOUT THE PENGUINS!

AND IT JUST BROKE MY HEART WHEN ONE OF THOSE PRECIOUS EGGS SLIPPED FROM THE CLUTCHES OF THEIR WEBBED FEET!

A LONELY EGG, LAYIN' ON THE FROZEN GROUND!

MY LIPS STILL QUIVER WHEN I THINK OF THE TRAGEDY...

AND IF NOBODY -SNIFF- WAS GONNA DO ANYTHING ABOUT IT...
HONK

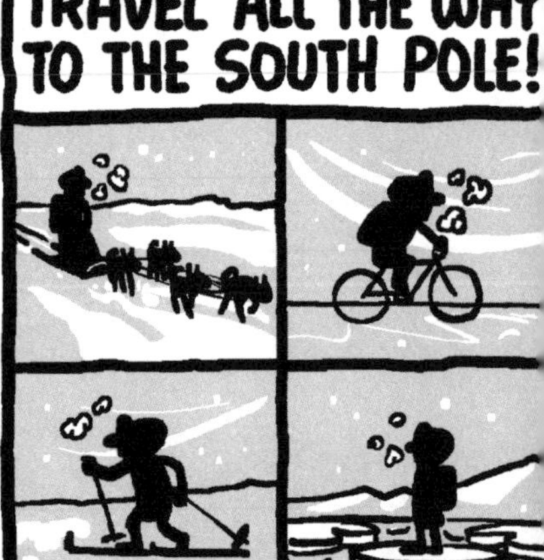

IT WAS UP TO ME TO TRAVEL ALL THE WAY TO THE SOUTH POLE!

I WAS DETERMINED TO INTERVENE WITH MOTHER NATURE AND STOP THE TRAGEDY!
BRUB-B-B-B-B-B-B

I WAS DETERMINED TO SAVE THOSE EGGS!
CLAP CLAP CLAP CLAP
CLAP CLAP CLAP

I MEAN, IT'S A TRAGEDY TO WASTE ALL THOSE EGGS!
Breakfast Special! PENGUIN EGGS!

WRITER AND ARTIST: ERIC SCOTT

Is it just us or are the standards for qualifying as human just a tad lower at game rooms? You look around and what do you see? Geeks, dweebs and pinheads walking from game to game with a fistful of quarters pretending they have a life! Yes, and every one of these pathetic losers has their place in MAD's gallery of...

Video Arcade Personalities

VOLUME I

WRITER: SEAN EISENPORTH
ARTIST: TOM BUNK

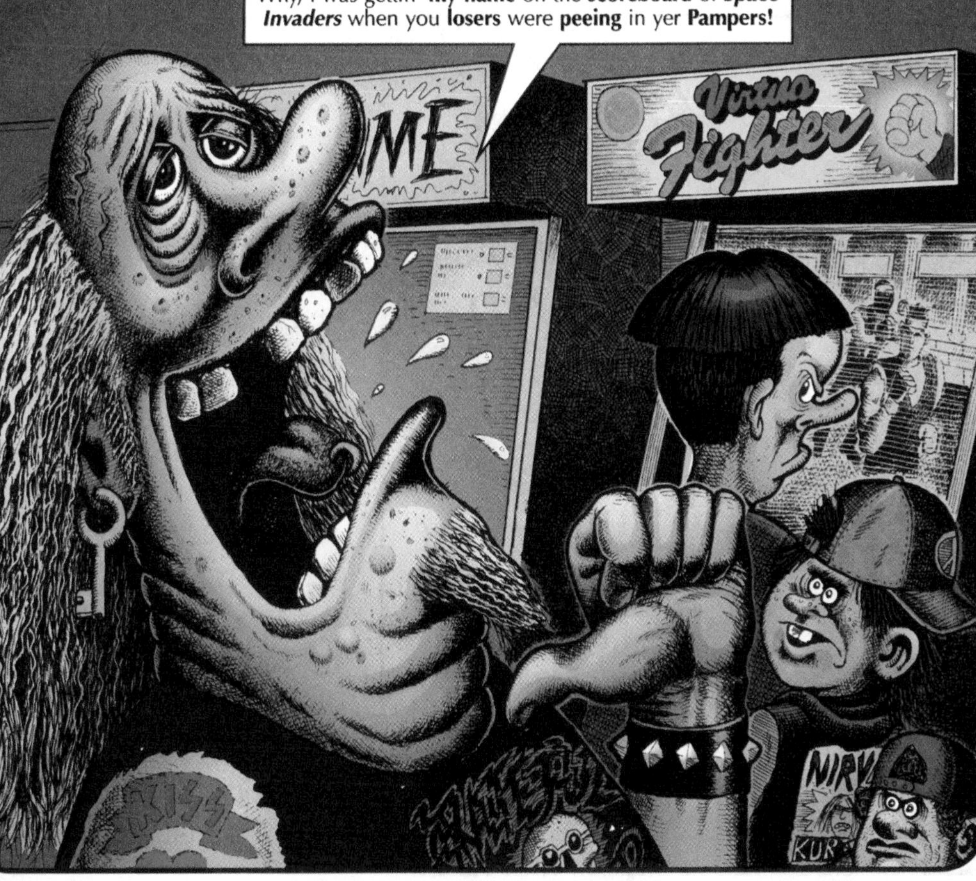

Aww shooot! *Virtua Fighter* is a game for little dinks! Why, I was gettin' my name on the scoreboard of *Space Invaders* when you losers were peeing in yer Pampers!
Virtua Fighter

THE VETERAN

Yeah yeah, The Veteran may have been a big shooter back in the ancient times of *Space Invaders* and *Asteroids*, but those days are long gone. Even so, that doesn't stop this legendary-blowhard/has-been from clinging desperately to his past and blabbering on about how cool he was back in 1981. Memo to The Veteran: No one gives a rat's butt!

Video Arcade Personalities

MR. NO-FRIENDS

Sure, you have to feel sorry for the guy, but whatever you do, don't make eye contact with Mr. No-Friends! If he starts yakking at you anyway, the best course of action is to just pretend you're deaf, because if you acknowledge him even once, he will stick to you like HERPES!

Yeah, so then I **found out** there's a **secret passage** on **Level 3** that lets you **WARP** directly into the **ZAP Dimension!** Like, it **should have** been **obvious,** right? But it **wasn't!** Hey, do **you** read ***Gamepro?*** I read ***Gamepro!*** I guess you can **tell, huh?**
DIE HARD
TOKENS 25¢ OR 3 for $ 1.00

THE GAME HOG

Not even a lengthy line-up of pissed-off homeboys can deter The Game Hog from monopolizing the hot, new game at the arcade. He continues to feed an endless supply of quarters into the slot, blissfully unaware of the hostility brewing behind his back. This explains why many Game Hogs never live to see their 21st birthday!

HE SUPER DADDY

He loves his kids — so much, in fact, that he takes them everywhere — even to the arcade! The Super Daddy does this because he's deeply committed to his child's personal growth and emotional development. That's why he sticks Junior between two video games for several hours — because it builds character!!

THE SCAVENGER

This pathetic loser carefully and systematically checks each and every machine coin return slot in a desperate search for unclaimed quarters. His ultimate gratification comes, however, when he finds a scoreboard where someone hasn't inserted their name. The Scavenger, of course, still lives at home with his parents!

COMING SOON...VOLUME II!

BIRTH OF A COMBINATION DEPT.

A few issues back we published a scathing indictment on the unimaginative film industry and its propensity to make sequel upon sequel upon sequel. We continue our puckish criticism of this horrendous practice with this sequel article...

MORE MOVI

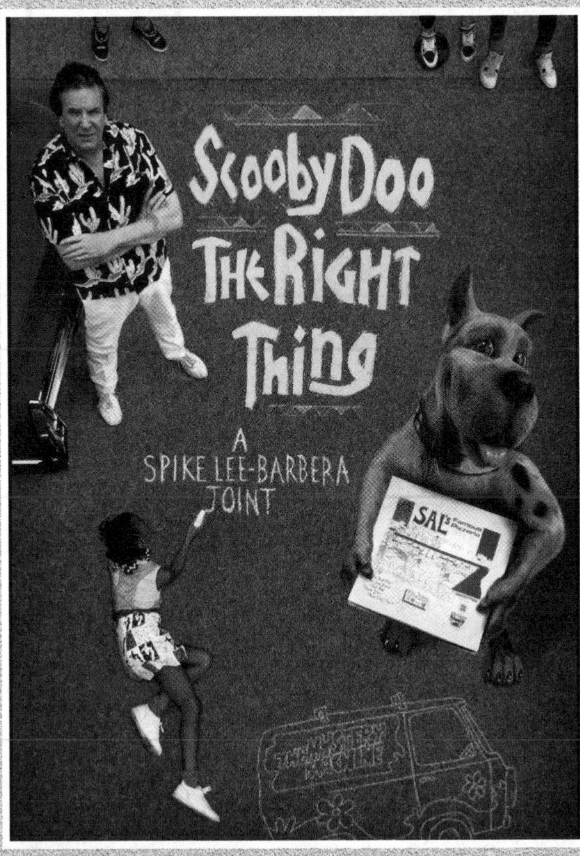

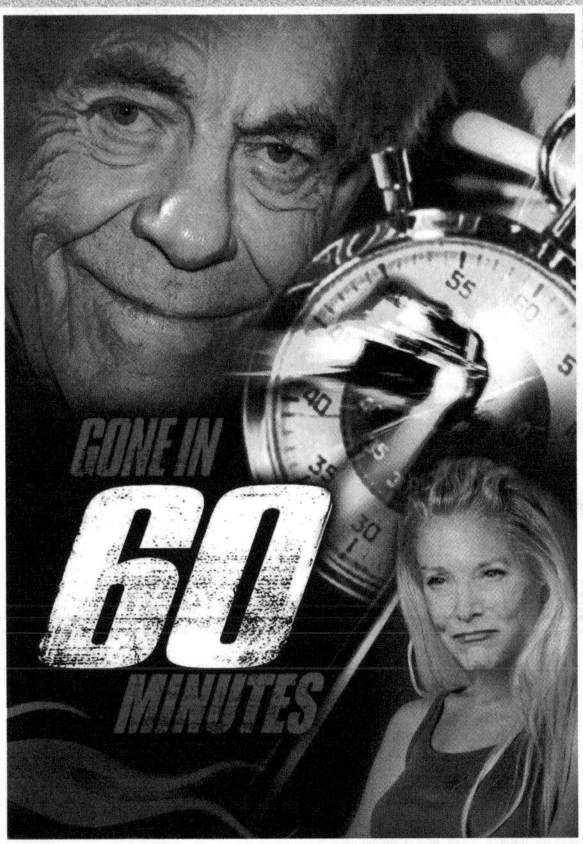

MASHUPS WE'D HATE TO SEE

D OF THE RINGS
ETURN OF THE King of QUEENS

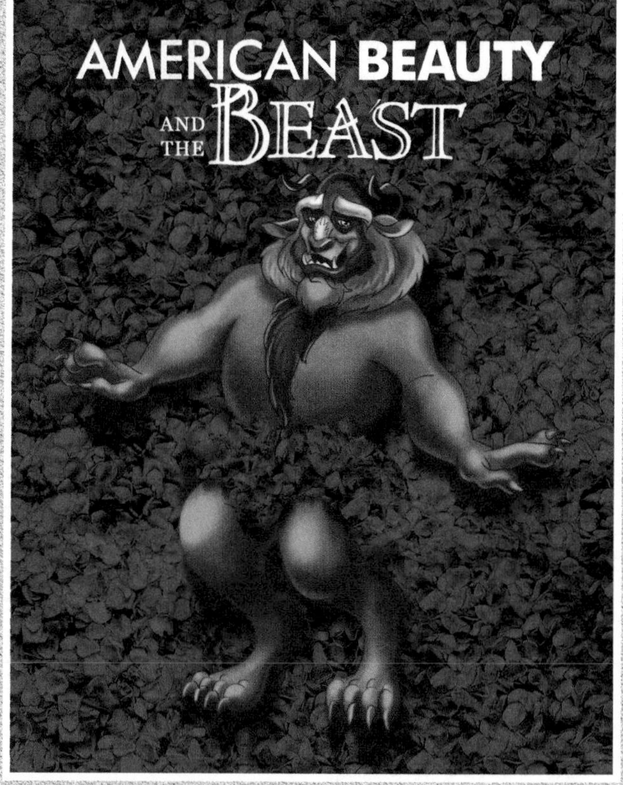

ARTIST: SCOTT BRICHER

THE HARDSHIP SUPER OF AMERICA'

THESE DAYS we hear a lot of alarming reports about overweight people. America, it seems, is a nation of fatties getting fatter all the time. But like most alarming reports from the media, you probably shouldn't believe them. The truth is, we've always been a country of overeating heifers, we just didn't have talking heads with hours of television airtime to get us all excited about them. Too bad! If we had TV back in the old West, we could have seen some pretty entertaining special reports, such as...

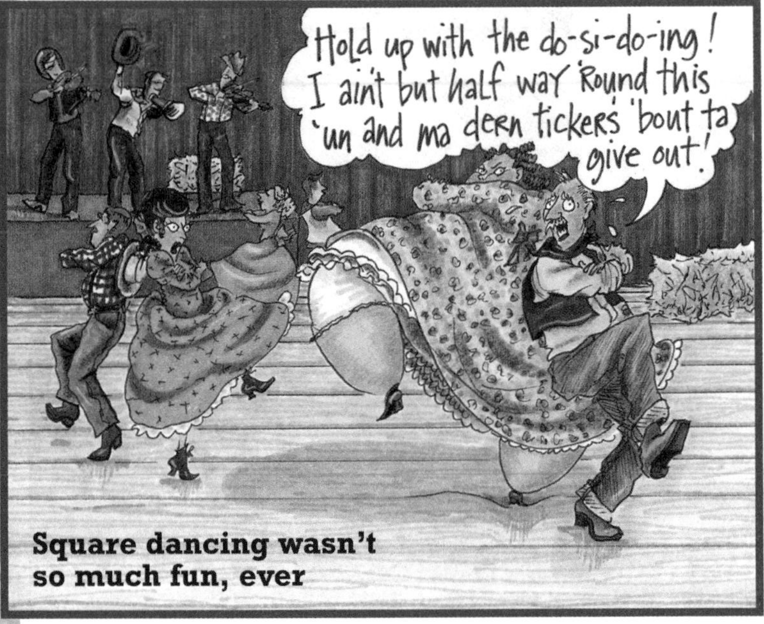

Square dancing wasn't so much fun, ever

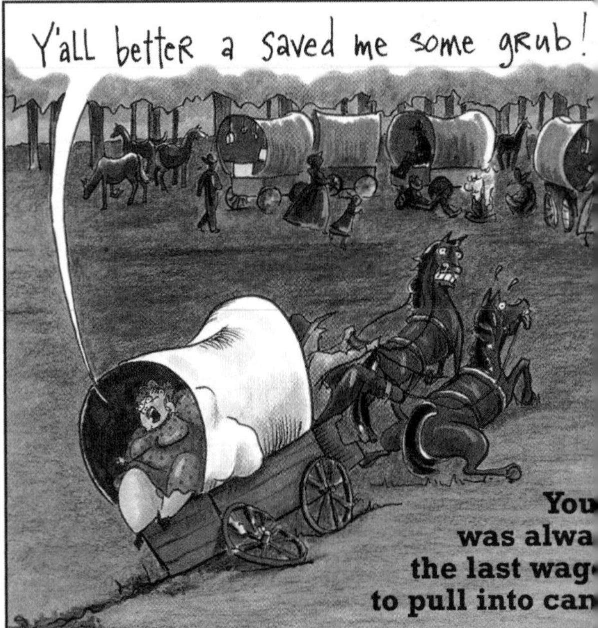

You was alwa the last wag to pull into can

The seldom-won quick-draw showdowns

Long, harsh winters left you feeling less like a person and more like a commodi

Gwan now, git under Lil' Debbie's free arm fer the night.

WRITER AND ARTIST: TERESA BURNS PARKHURST

ACED BY THE OBESE WILD WEST

Even the best-made chaps were never slimming

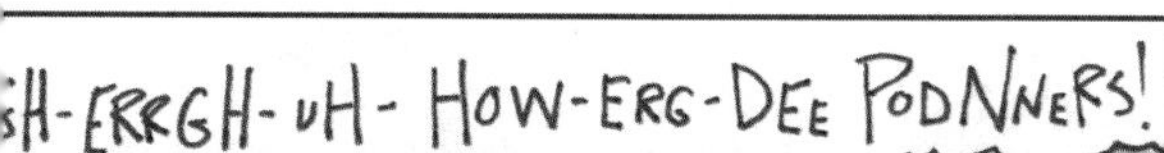

ou were ever, ever icked for e posse

o matter that ey swung wide, aloon doors were constant struggle

Support groups were hard to come by

Being the only one to survive an Indian attack was pretty embarrassing

MAD PRESENTS OTHER USES FOR LOB

DIAPER RINSER

EARPHONES HOLDER

COAT & HAT RACK

TURN SIGNAL

LIVE
STERS

PAPER TOWEL RACK

BIRD FEEDER

ITEM GRABBER

CORN HOLDER

DESK SET

WRITER AND ARTIST: PAUL PETER PORGES

CANDLE HOLDER

PIZZA PIE SLICER

ELECTRICIAN'S WIRESTRIPPER

MUSIC STAND

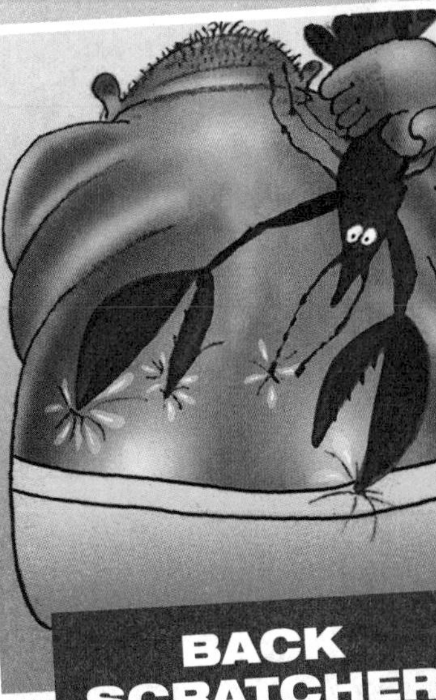
BACK SCRATCHER

WOOL SOCKS DRYER

TOOTHBRUSH HOLDER

JOKE AND DAGGER DEPT.

WRITER AND ARTIST: ANTONIO PROHIAS COLORIST: CARRIE STRACHAN

THAT DIDN'T MAK

CRUSTY

The Cookie and Chips Crumbs-Filled, Soda Spill-Stained Minivan

LUKE WARM

The Always-Late Pizza Delivery Car

MUGGY

The Hot, Noisy, Squeaky Summer Camp Bus

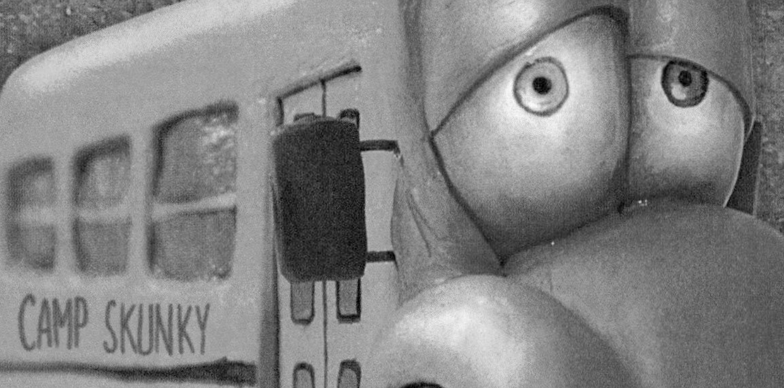

PERCY

The Soap Box Derby Show-off

WRITER: JACOB LAMBERT SCULPTOR: LIZ LOMAX

…T INTO THE MOVIE!

FRANK

The Greasy, Dirty, Bug-Infested Hot Dog Wagon

LURCH

The Impossible-To-Steer Bumper Car

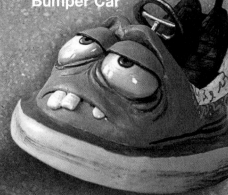

MR. SPEEDEE

The Too-Fast Ice Cream Truck

SQUEALER

The Loud, Gas-Smelling, Always Comes In Last Go-Kart

GALACTICKLE DEPT.
IN A GALAXY MILLIONS OF LIGHT YEARS AWAY, A BAD EVIL GALACTIC EMPIRE HAS PLANS FOR A SUPER SPACE STATION THAT CAN DESTROY AN ENTIRE PLANET. LED BY GOOD PRINCESS LAIDUP, REBEL FORCES STEAL THE PLANS...AND A MIGHTY STAR WAR TAKES
evil Galactic Empire . . . **killing** and **destroying** everything in sight!!
Hey, clue me in . . . How do we tell the **GOOD GUYS** from the **BAD GUYS** around here, anyway?!
Simple! The **WHITES** are **BAD!** The **BLACKS** are **GOOD!**
Where'd they **get that** idea from, **Ganoomo Sajo** . . . the ruler of **Mars?**
No, **Muhammad Ali** . . . the ruler of **Earth!**
If us **BAD** guys are in **WHITE,** and the **GOOD** guys are in **BLACK** . . . what's our **Leader** doing dressed in **Black . . .?**
You may not **believe** this, but he hasn't changed his costume in **20 years!** It **started OUT white,** but with all his **dirty work . . .**
You are now in my **power,** Princess Laidup! Return the **plans** you stole, and I'll make **it worth** your **while!**
You can't bribe **me,** Zader! You **forget,** I'm **fearless** and **honest** and **decent** and **incor-ruptible!**
Come on! Where are the **plans?**
If you **must** know, I gave them to a pair of **robots!**

edible! Our goes faster the speed of t, and our fire almost fast as the ed of light!
Yeah . . . so guess what just happened! We shot ourselves down!!
What?! You mean to tell me that the In-Flight Movie is Bugs Bunny chasing the Roadrunner up a hill?!?
What do you expect on a seven second flight . . . "The Godfather"?
How high up into space would you say this ship goes?
Quiet! I'm about to say a prayer before we go into battle . . .
OUR FATHER WHO ART BELOW US IN HEAVEN—
That high, huh?
Boy, these space ships are noisy!! Maybe that's why they call this movie . . .
STAR ROARS
ARTIST: HARRY NORTH, ESQ.
WRITER: LARRY SIEGEL WITH DICK DE BARTOLO
got away, -Stool! So so good! Princess ends on us! r mission st not fail!
Beedeep! Boop! Tweet!
TRANSLATION: If we're both robots, Cree-Pio, how come we look—and talk—so different?
Because I happen to be a magnificent, articulate golden Adonis, and you're a sawed-off, incoherent, stupid sack of bolts!
Beedeep! Boop!
TRANSLATION: I knew there had to be a scientific reason for it!
ESCAP CAPSU C
Goodness gracious, this planet simply screams for some—Je ne sais quoi—in the way of decor! Still, in some ways, it's a veritable Shangri-La! Take my hand, Bar-Stool . . . I'm a stranger in paradise . . .
Beedeep! Tweet!
TRANSLATION: As if I don't have enough problems, now I'm stuck with a gay robot!
-Stool, we seem to lost! Oh, dear . . . k what's coming! endish creatures ut to tear us limb limb and commit speakable acts of elty upon us . . . !
Follow the yellow sand road! Follow the yellow sand road! Follow . . . follow . . . follow . . . follow . . . Follow the yellow sand road!
Beep! Zit! Gack!
TRANSLATION: And then again . . . there's an outside chance they may be Space Munchkins!
Hi, strangers! I'm Lube Skystalker! I'm a senior at Buffoin Tech, where I major in Incredible Space Heroics!
Gracious, there couldn't be any money in THAT field!
You're telling me! That's why I'm minoring in Space Accounting! Hey, anyone ever tell you you look like an "Oscar"?!?
Take a good look! With your performance in this film, it's as close as you'll ever get to an Academy Award!

We need help! It's our Princess! She's in terrible trouble! I'm now going to press a button on my companion here, and an image will appear with a message that may mean life or death for the entire universe! Here goes . . .
Welcome to "Hollywood Squares"!
Whoops! Wrong button! Don't tell me you get THAT thing up here too!
Yep! There's no way you can keep it out!

Ah, here's the Princess now!
Save me, Oldie Von Moldie . . . wherever you are! You are my only hope! Otherwise, millions of people will be wiped out in a holocaust, the likes of which civilization has never seen!
Is that her whole bit? Just that?
No, actually she closes with a saxophone solo that'll blow your mind! But you get the idea! Lube, you must help us find Oldie Von Moldie!
Hop in my space car!

Look! There's Oldie Von Moldie!! Many years ago, my Father and he were Military Pilots together! Now, he's 97 . . . he can hardly see . . . and his hands shake terribly!
What does he do now?
What else? He's a Commercial Airlines Pilot!

Oldie, Princess Laidup is in the hands of that rat, Zader! We haven't a moment to lose!
Eh? What's that? You say you want to go up to my flat later and sing the blues??
He doesn't seem to HEAR too well, either!
In his spare time, he moonlights as a Telephone Operator!

Very well, Lube! We will go into town, find us a space ship and rescue Princess Laidup!
But first, I must teach you about the Force . . .
The Force? what's that?!?
It is a Power that is all around us! It is everywhere at all times! It knows all and sees all! It is eternal!
They have something like that on Earth! It's called "The Internal Revenue Service"!

Hold it! Let me see your I.D.!
He doesn't have to show you his I.D.!
He doesn't have to show me his I.D.!
He can go about his business!
He can go about his business!
Gee, Oldie, how did you do that?
The Force gives you power over weak minds!
The Force gives me power over weak minds!
All right! Drive on!
All right! Drive on!

I can't go home, Zfrx! My gargoyle doesn't understand me!
Who in heck are you?
Does the name Quasimodo ring a bell?
Funny! This is what I usually see in a bar AFTER I've had a few drinks!
What's so special about this place? It looks like any Singles Bar in any big city on Earth!
I've had too much to drink! I'm seeing weird things!
This bar is FULL of weird things!!
I'm talking about those human forms that just came in! Man, those are WEIRD THINGS!!

How fast?
28,000 REPTMS per hour!
How fast is that!
More than twice as fast as 11,000 REPTMS per hour!
Wow! That IS fast! Okay . . . we'll take it!

I can let you have this baby on our Seven Day Special! No daily charges, we supply the fuel, and you can drop it off at any planet! Let's see . . . at 15c a mile . . . for your trip . . . it will cost you . . . TOPS . . . 600 million bucks!
WHAT? That's preposterous! It's insane!
Boy, you sure drive a hard bargain! Okay, okay! I'll throw in the $2.50 Collision Insurance!
I knew he'd come around!!

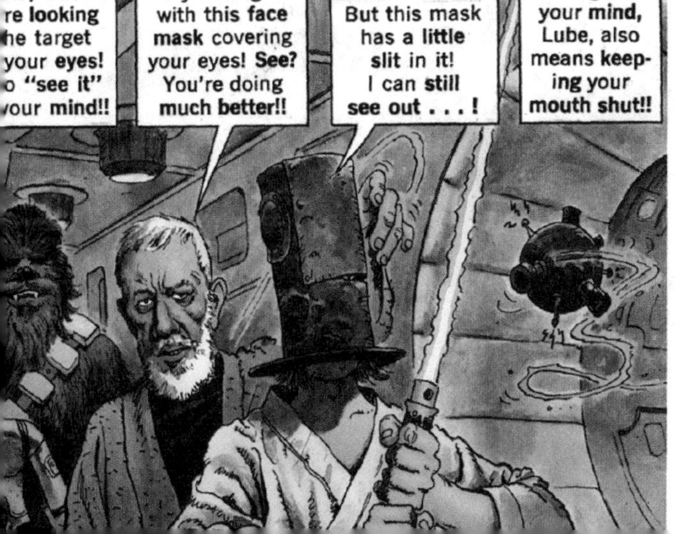
Try hitting it with this face mask covering your eyes! See? You're doing much better!!
But this mask has a little slit in it! I can still see out . . . !
Seeing with your mind, Lube, also means keeping your mouth shut!!

I hope you guys don't mind my bringing Chewbacco along as my co-pilot!
Wow! This has been one weird trip so far . . . hasn't it, Oldie?
Well, when someone piloting a ship I'm on starts pounding his chest, climbing the walls and eating bananas, I worry!!
Me too! And there's no telling what the APE is liable to do, either!

Princess Laidup, you are a prisoner aboard the most **advanced space ship** in **history!** It has **fire power** strong enough to wipe out **any planet!** It has **speed** enough to wipe out **any enemy!** And it has a **Symphony Orchestra** loud enough to wipe out **any audience!** Now watch as we destroy that **planet** ahead!
Excuse me, but I'm from the **Electric Company . . .** and **before** you wipe out any more planets, you'll have to pay your **bill!** You owe us **$4 million** in **back payments,** and **that's** just for **YESTERDAY!!**
BILL FINAL DEMAND FOR WASTING RIGA IV ... $4,000,000

I suddenly feel a **sick sensation** in my stomach . . . like a million souls crying out in terror! It's . . . an **incredible disturbance,** I feel . . .
Perhaps the Death Ship has blown up an **entire planet . . . ?**
Perhaps .
Then aga
it might
the **radish**
I had fo
lunch . .

Look! It's the evil Galactic Empire **Death Ship Space Station . . .** straight ahead of us!
Let's **get out** of here!
We **can't!** We've **lost control!** We're being **drawn toward it!** They have their X-5-G Nuclear Hoover-Matic on **"Full Suck"!!**

I've got **good** news and **bad** news! First, the **bad** news! That Death Ship **Space Port** is jammed with **50,000 heavily armed bad guys!**
Gulp! What's the **GOOD NEWS?**
We proba
won't ha
to go
throug
Baggag
Claim!

Remember, lads, try to act **nonchalant!**
Anybody come by your **post,** Zargg?
Yeah! A party of **six!** Two guys, a 97-year-old man, a couple of robots, and a 14-foot ape!
Okay . . . but if you see anything **UNUSUAL,** let me know!

Here's my **first plan,** men! **You** fellows . . . take over the **Control Room** and rescue the **Princess . . .** and **I'll** take care of **Zader!!**
Look, Oldie! The ba
guys have **spotted** u
Okay . . . here's my **second** plan . . . **RUN LIKE HELL!!**

Your Highness, I'm Lube Skystalker! I'm majoring in "Incredible Space Heroics" at Buffooin Tech! As my Term Project, I decided to organize an army, find a convenient space ship, rescue you, and fly you six billion miles to safety on the planet, Draidel!
This is madness! You know what happens if you fail?!
Don't even mention it! God . . . who wants to be a Space Accountant!
PLEASE KNOCK AND ENTER

BEWARE OF DOG
And what is your reason for doing it, Mr. Yoyo . . . ?
Princess, I'm doing it for the money!!
Then I will see to it that you get plenty! I will give you $20 million!
Wow! Just think of what I can buy with $20 million!
Well, if you go to Earth, you can buy a tank of gas for $20 million! This is 2012, you know...!

What fantastic luck! Who arranged for you to carry a handy rope on your belt with a hook that happens to fit over that projection so we can swing over this bottomless pit?
Probably the same clever guy who saw to it that 500 sharpshooters could fire at us and miss from a distance of ten feet!

What's happening? Where are we? The walls are starting to close in!!
Great!! We're not only in the world's largest Space Station . . . we're also in the world's largest Trash Compactor!
Well, at least they won't find us here!
And if they DO find us, they won't recognize us! They'll be looking for FULL-SIZED people!!

So, Zader! We meet again! Prepare your Light Ray Sword for a duel to the death! I shall triumph because I have The Force!
Get ready to die, you black-hearted villain!!
Good lord! My light ray has gone out!!
How ironic! Betrayed by a lack of faith in The Force . . .
. . . and a ridiculously short . . . gasp . . . extension cord!

Well . . . you did it! You rescued me, you beat up on the bad guys, and now you are about to receive a hero's welcome here on Draidel!
Hello, people of Draidel . . . !

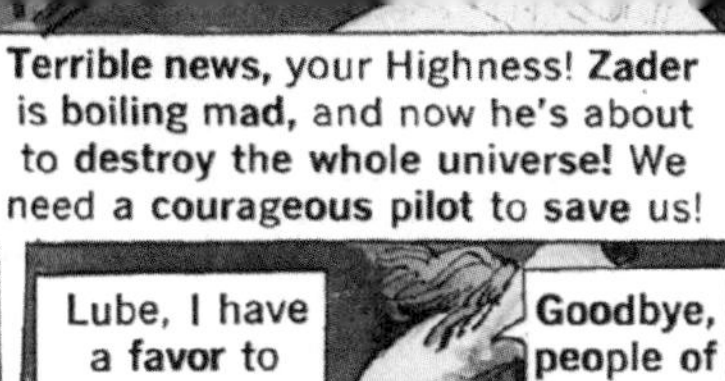

Terrible news, your Highness! Zader is boiling mad, and now he's about to destroy the whole universe! We need a courageous pilot to save us!

Lube, I have a favor to ask you . . .
Goodbye, people of Draidel!

The enemy is breaking through our defenses, Sir! They're using small one-man ships! We never planned on being attacked by anything that small!
I can't believe
We build the
advanced space
in history, and
body thought
putting
on the

Remember, I am with you, Lube!
I know that, Oldie!
Do you feel my presence!
More than that, I feel your weight!
So will you please get off my space ship! It's only built for one . . . and you're going to make me crash!
Besides, time is running out! We must penetrate their defenses, enter the target shaft, and fire on the exact spot that will start a chain reaction!
But how will you know where that exact spot is?
It's a one in a billion chance!!

Wait a minute . . . !! That may JUST be it!!
THIS WAY
TO DESTROY EVIL GALACTIC EMPIRE

KER-
BOOM
TINKLE TINKLE

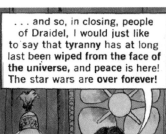

. . . and so, in closing, people of Draidel, I would just like to say that tyranny has at long last been wiped from the face of the universe, and peace is here! The star wars are over forever!
But . . . that's terrible! That's simply awful!!

Now that we've made the universe safe, we've opened it up for the tourists!!
WA-AL!
SA-AY!
WHERE CAN I GET A DECENT FRANK
EAT YOUR HEART OUT DISNEY PLANET!
GEE
...LOUSY BEDS!
MOM, I WANNA THROW U—
Y'MEAN THE BROAD'S A REAL PRINCESS?!
BURP

Fairy Tale
SCENES WE'D LIKE TO SEE
THE FROG PRINCE

WRITER AND ARTIST: DON MARTIN

JOHN CALDWELL'S

13 THINGS YOU REALLY LEARN

You thought you could just skate right through the school year, that you'd be able to do a minimal amount of work and the teachers would pass you on to the next grade — boy, were you wrong, moron! Now it's time to pay the price! So say goodbye to fun in the sun and hello to long days in hot classrooms. It's going to be bad — *really* bad — as you will see in...

1

Anybody can suck at math, but it takes a real dipwad to be taking shop class over.

2

TODAY, WE'RE GOING TO STUDY THE ISOSCELES TRIANGLE!

The really good teachers, like the really good students, don't end up in summer school.

3

Crib notes, cheat sheets and ballpoint answer tattoos are harder to hide under light summer clothing.

4

BUZZ BUZZ BUZZ, ADJECTIVES, B
BUZZ BUZZA, PREDICATES, BUZZ
BUZZA BUZZ BUZZ, NOUNS, BU
BUZZ DANGLING PARTICIPLES.

Teachers tend to drone on much longer when there aren't any wiseguy know-it-alls there to raise their hands every ten seconds.

ARTIST AND WRITER: JOHN CALDWELL COLORIST: CARRIE STRA

SUMMER SCHOOL

5
...AND SO, ACCORDING TO BOTH OF YOU GENTLEMEN, THE CAPITOL OF DENMARK IS WICHITA?

When it comes to copying answers on tests, the pickings can be quite slim.

HARPER LOOKS IN FOR THE SIGN... DOOLEY TAKES A LEAD OFF THIRD... 3 AND 2 COUNT ON THE BATTER... WITH TWO OUT AND THE TYING RUN ON SECOND...

So-called "classic literature" written by dead glish guys is just as difficult to get through dur-ng baseball season as it is in football season.

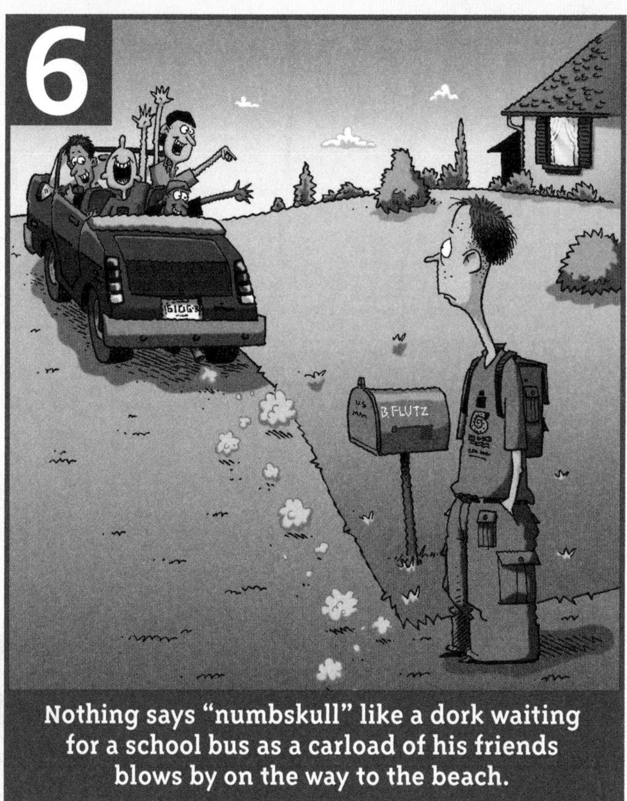

Nothing says "numbskull" like a dork waiting for a school bus as a carload of his friends blows by on the way to the beach.

Unlike the rest of the year, breaking up into teams for a science project doesn't mean there'll be at least one smart kid there to help jackup your grades.

9
WHAT WAS THE ORIGINAL CAPITAL OF THE UNITED STATES OF AMERICA?
CAPITAL T!!
ABOUT NINE BUCKS AND A BEAVER PELT!
WASHINGTON A. C.!
HOBOKEN, OLD JERSEY!!
HOW ABOUT YOUR— EEH... WHATEVER

Trying to be the class clown in a roomful of other slacker jokesters is just not worth the effort.

Everybody can't sit in the last row.

Fewer students on the bus means that it's harder to avoid the bullies.

There's nothing lower on the culinary ladder than substitute summer lunch ladies.

13

UM... WOULD YOU LIKE UM... FRIES WITH THAT?

The upside of the whole thing is that it means one less menial and humiliating minimum wage summer job that you have to put on your resume.

ESSAY TOPICS GUARANTEED TO LAND YOU IN SUMMER SCHOOL

- RING AND RUN: A SCIENTIFIC STUDY OF DOORBELLS
- CAPS I HAVE WORN BACKWARDS (A SHOW AND TELL PROJECT)
- GROWING GYM SOCK FUNGUS: A FIELD GUIDE TO SUCCESS
- KLINGON GRAFFITI AN UNRECOGNIZED CAREER OPPORTUNITY
- CHUGGING SLURPEES AND ITS EFFECT ONNNNNN TTHHHHE BRAAAAINININ

TALES FROM the DUCK SIDE SLITHERING HEIGHTS

ARTIST AND WRITER: DUCK EDWING COLORIST: CARRIE STRACHAN

Planet TAD!!!!!

Planet TAD!!!!!

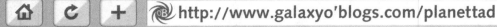

[**About Me**]

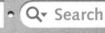

[**Name**|Tad]
[**Grade**|9]
[**Monkeys or Apes?**|Monkeys]

[15 February|**03:19pm**]

[**mood**| 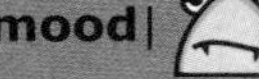 bored]

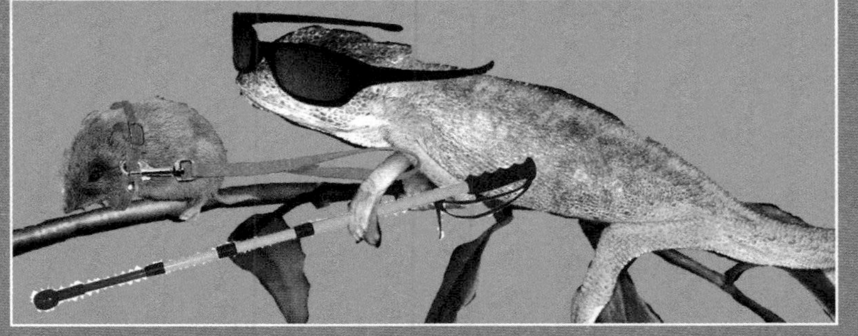

In my biology textbook, I read that even blind chameleons change color to match their surroundings. I asked my dad how they figured that out, and he said, "Well, I guess they did a study where they blinded some chameleons and then saw what happened."

I think it's weird that somewhere out there in the world, there's a guy whose job title is: Chameleon Blinder.

I wonder how you know when you've successfully blinded a chameleon. Do you ask it how many fingers you're holding up? Or what?

[15 February|**06:41pm**]

I've been thinking about it, and if I ever have a band, it will be called Blind Chameleon.

[16 February|**05:50pm**]

[**mood**|  impatient]

My birthday is now six days away. The number of days until I can drive can now be measured in mere hundreds. I pointed that out to my mom today, and she said, "I'll savor every one of them."

Mom's sarcastic sometimes.

[17 February|**03:36pm**]

Chuck Wiggins brought his Nintendo DS to school today. He let me see it. That's all he let me do, though — see it. He wouldn't let me hold it, because, he said, "My mom said I can't let people play with it, because they might break it. Plus, it's flu season, so it's better not to touch things other people have touched." (Chuck's a nice guy, but his mom's super-nervous about everything, and as a result, so's he. Until he was in sixth grade, she made Chuck wear a helmet on the school bus.)

The Nintendo DS is pretty cool — it's got a program that makes it look like it's got a puppy inside it, and you can make it fetch and stay and stuff. Chuck really likes it because his mom won't let him have a dog, because she's afraid it might one day go crazy and kill

[**mood**| hungry]

If you think about it, "tater tot" is a bad name for a food, because it suggests that you're eating potato babies.

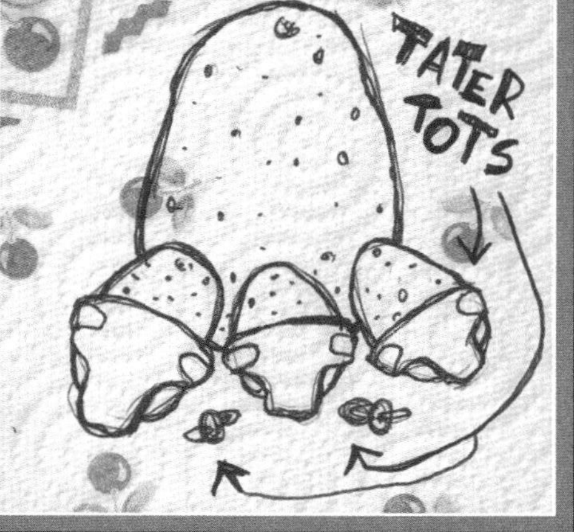

[**mood**| envious]

I really need a Nintendo DS. In study hall today, Chuck and my friend Darren were sitting on opposite sides of the room, racing against each other on Mario Kart on their DS-es. I had nothing to do but draw baby potato angels.

[21 February|**03:43pm**]

[**mood**| anxious]

At breakfast, I reminded my mom and dad that I want a Nintendo DS for my birthday. And my mom said, "Well, maybe if you're good, you'll get that GameBoy you want." And I got all worried and said, "No! I want a DS! Why did you think I wanted a GameBoy? I have a GameBoy!" And she said, "Oh, a DS? Well, it's probably too late to get you one of those." And then she smiled at my dad. So I think they're just messing with my head.

At least, I really hope that's all they're doing.

[22 February|**06:50am**]

[**mood**| birthday]

I got a Nintendo DS! Can't blog now — I'm teaching Chuckbiter to fetch.

[28 February|**07:26pm**]

[**mood**| devastated]

Bad news. I went over to Chuck's today, and Darren came over, and we were all playing with our DS-es. And then I put my DS on the floor and went to the kitchen to get a soda, and then, when I came back, I stepped on it and broke it.

I don't even know what was worse — breaking my DS, or having Chuck's mom come in the room immediately afterward and say, "You see, Chuck? That's why you shouldn't let Tad touch your things."

WRITER: TIM CARVELL ARTIST: BRIAN DURNIAK

ONE DAY IN THE COUNTRY

WRITER: CHARLIE KADAU ARTIST: DON MARTIN

If you like THIS BOOK,
a younger reader you know is sure to like our
DELIGHTFUL ANIMAL BOOKS
shown on the following pages!

Don't be afraid to ask for them by name!
Thank You!

BAD DOG, CARL

By Alexandra Stray

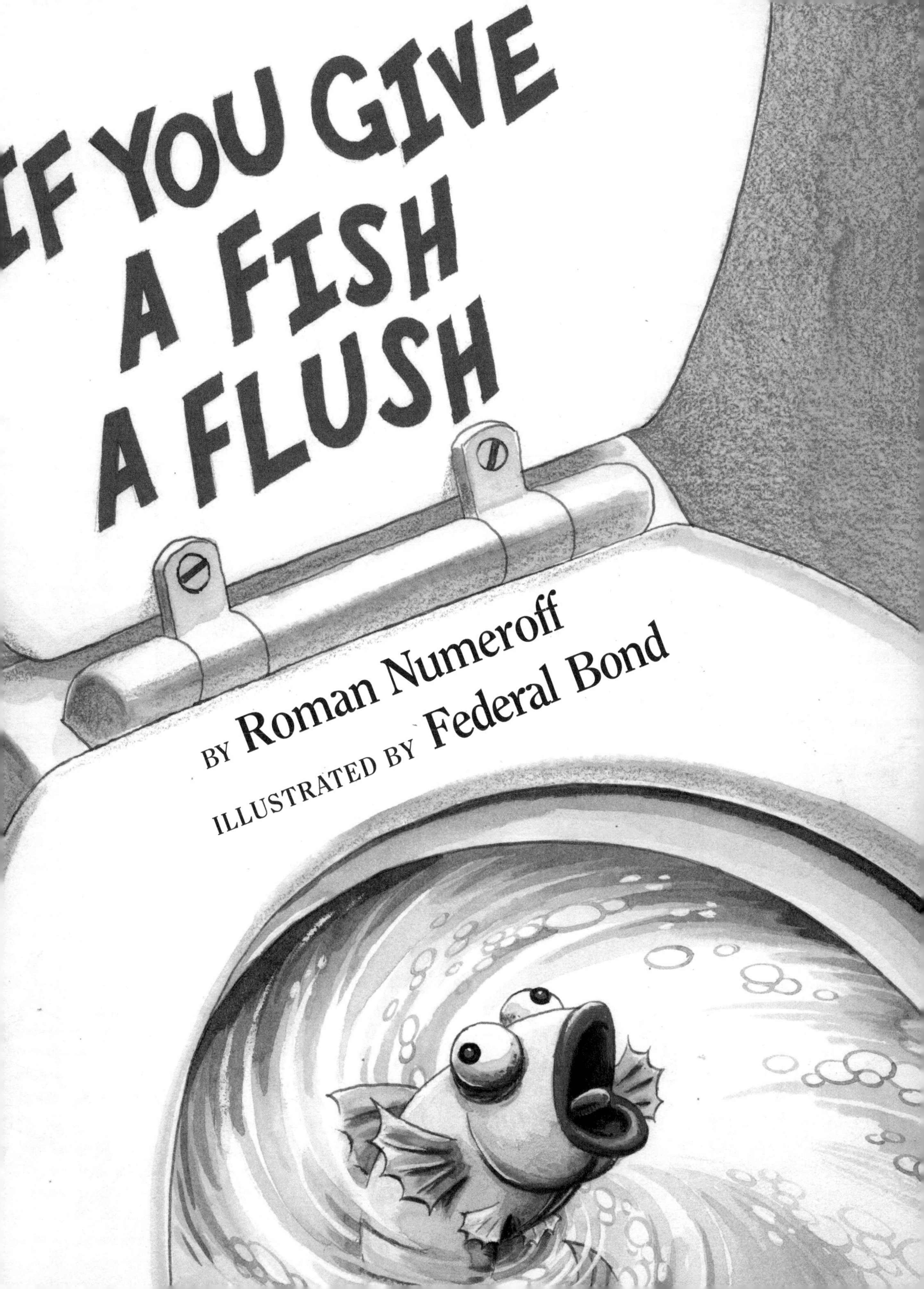
IF YOU GIVE
A FISH
A FLUSH
BY Roman Numeroff
ILLUSTRATED BY Federal Bond

Dizzy's

Winnie the Poo

FRESH AROMA

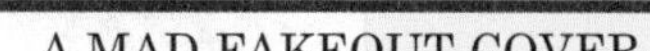
A MAD FAKEOUT COVER

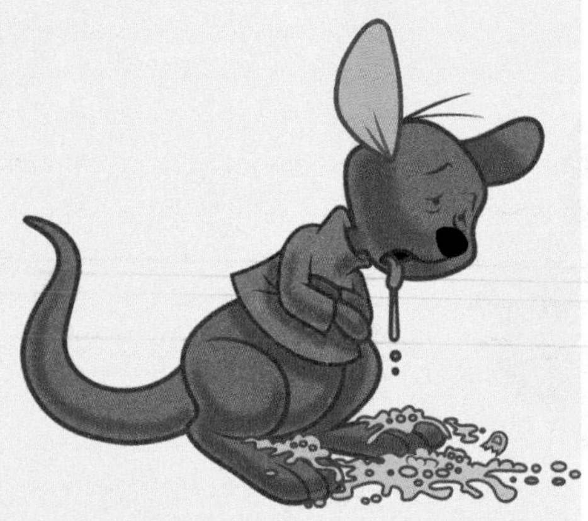

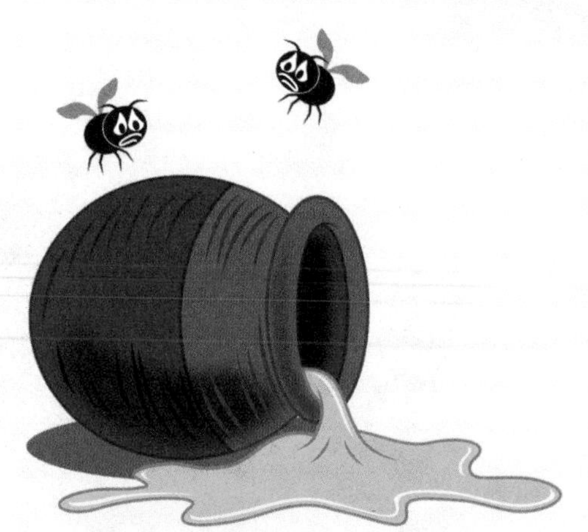

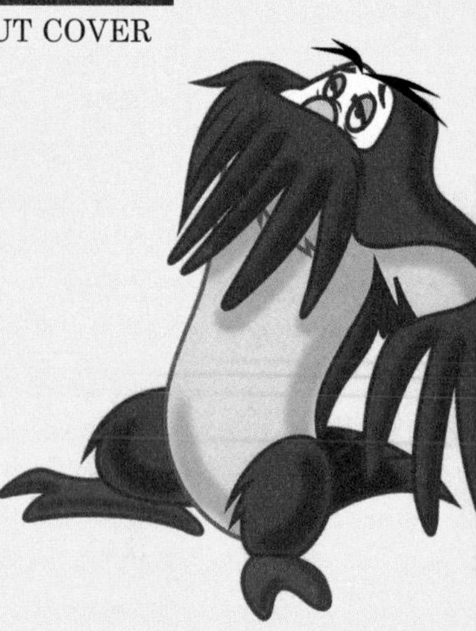

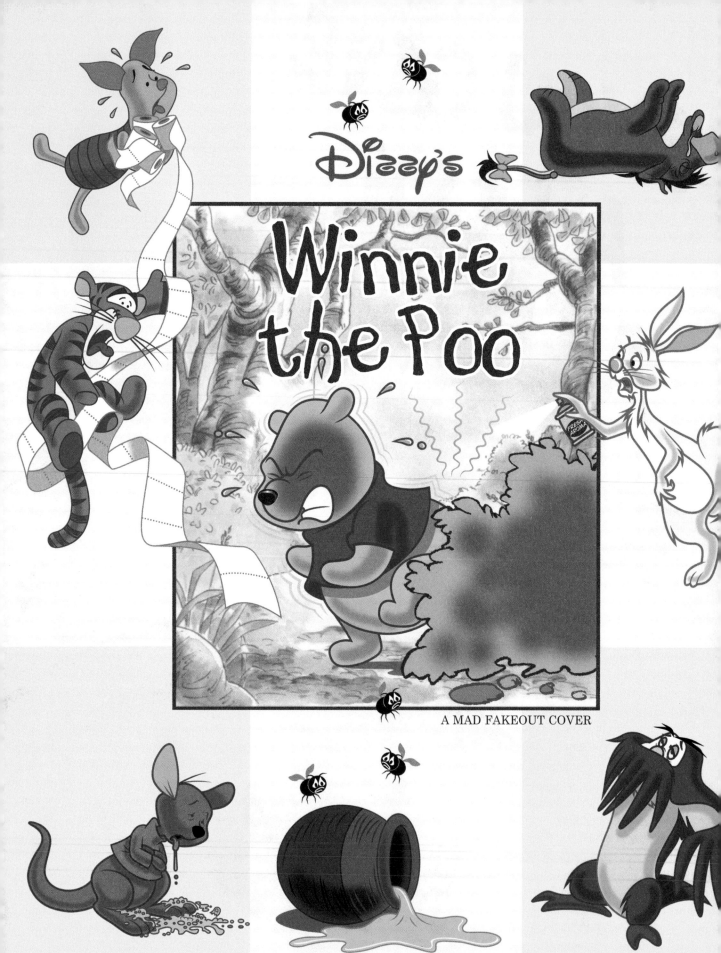

JOKE AND DAGGER DEPT.

SPY VS SPY VS SPY

WRITER AND ARTIST: ANTONIO PROHIAS COLORIST: CARRIE STRACHAN

The Eye of a Kitten

My name is Joe and I've been a Chicago fireman for almost five months now. In that time you could say I've seen it all. I've seen buildings on fire. I've seen buildings NOT on fire. I've seen things on fire I swear I didn't think could even catch on fire. I've seen "safety" matches that, frankly, didn't look all that "safe." But nothing prepared me for seeing an overcrowded nursing home on fire with an adorable litter of kittens, all confused and scared, trapped inside!

There's more to being a fireman than racing through red lights, squirting water into windows and chopping down doors.

It's called saving lives.

But is a human's life more important than a kitten's? I don't know; that wasn't on the firemen's test. But I know how I felt when I looked in the window and through the smoke saw all those elderly people in a panic, every one of them capable of stepping right on one of those little, defenseless, darling kittens.

I smashed a window, sending glass everywhere. As I went to pick up their cardboard home, it crumbled in my hands. I grabbed a fire helmet from a colleague who had collapsed nearby and I used it as a basket for them. Then outside, I jumped into the closest truck, turned on the siren, and drove north, where I remembered there was a veterinarian's office.

I rushed in and handed over the kittens to one of the several vets sitting around the reception area. I didn't have to say anything; my gear and expression said it all and they sprang into action.

Nervously, I paced for what seemed like hours. Finally, a vet emerged and asked me how I wanted to pay for this. I told him we'd charge it to the county.

"In that case, we better do more testing," he winked and added, "You go home and get some rest; you can't do any good here."

What good could I do at home? I'd just worry myself sick to the point of vomiting. But I did go home for a change of clothes and, sure enough, I vomited on them before I could get into them.

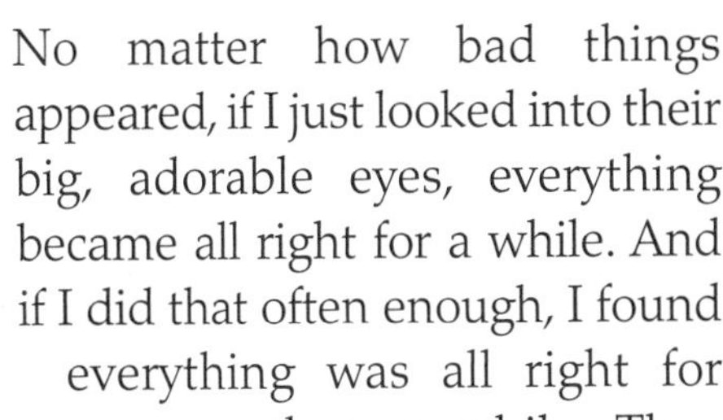

There were a number of messages on my answering machine. Most were from the Chief, who wanted to know where I was and what I did with the hook and ladder. Some folks just aren't cat people and you-know-who, I'm afraid, is one of them. I'd call him later; I didn't want to tie up my phone in case the doctors needed to reach me with some urgent, early test results.

For the next two weeks I practically lived in their reception area, praying for their recovery. At last the test results came: there was a piece of glass in a paw of one kitten, several of them had been dehydrated, and all of them had become addicted to pain killers, but overall, it was good news.

I didn't realize that each of the kittens had been assigned their own night nurse but that sure explained why the bill was almost six figures.

Since their other "home" was burnt to a crisp, I realized I now had 7 new "roommates."

When we got home, I was surprised to learn there was a warrant out for my arrest. It was then I realized that these fuzzy treasures had a special gift to give me.

No matter how bad things appeared, if I just looked into their big, adorable eyes, everything became all right for a while. And if I did that often enough, I found everything was all right for more than a while. They were magical hours that turned into magical days. Then magical weeks soon followed.

Try it and see for yourself. It's what I have come to call the Miracle of the Kittens. But before that, I called it Kitty-time in Blissville. I'd tried Felines in Funtown – that was okay for a while, but then it started to annoy me. Puttie Tats in Wonderland actually angered me, but I used it anyway. Then there's Cutie-Pies from Kremulon, which is a distant planet I travel to when things get weird on Earth and I get the feeling my head is going to start changing shape again.

I'm going to take the kitties with me next time.

— Joe the Fireman
(Temporarily on Indefinite Suspension)

WRITER: BRIAN MCCONNACHIE
ARTIST: LEONARDO RODRIGUEZ

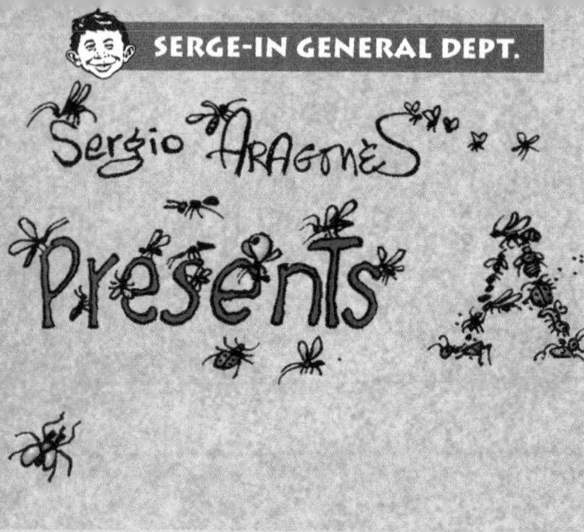
Sergio Aragonés
Presents

A MAD LOO

ACME EXTERMINATOR
PEST CONTROL
FLIT
OJAI TERMITE AND PEST CONTROL

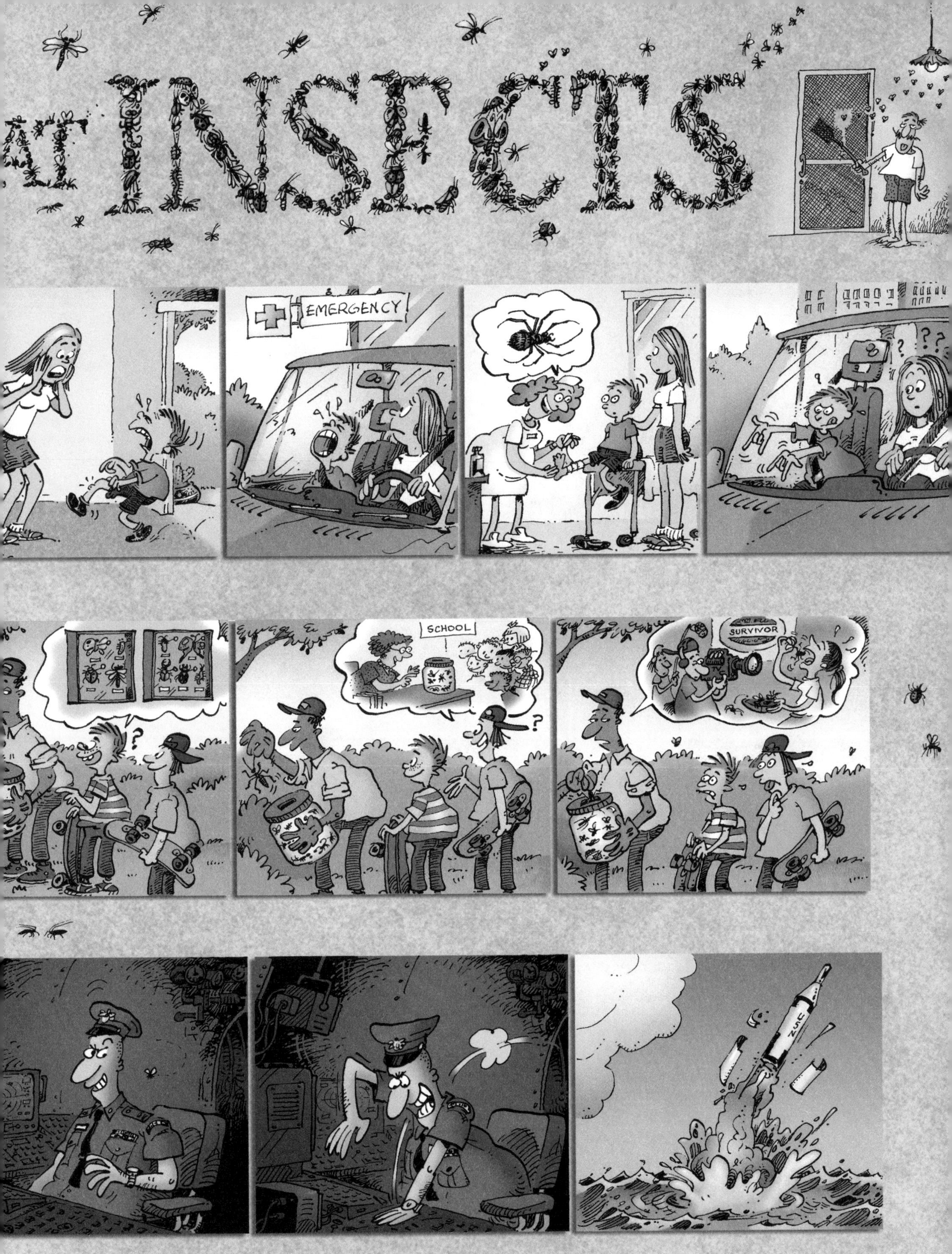

INSECTS

WRITER AND ARTIST: SERGIO ARAGONES COLORIST: TOM LUTH

ONE SATURDAY AFTERNOON DOWNTOWN

WRITER AND ARTIST: DON MARTIN COLORIST: CARL PETERSON

WHEELY PISSED OFF DEPT.

So you're in a vicious battle with your sworn enemies for the fate of the universe, a million miles away from your home planet of Cybertron and facing death at every turn. Sounds tough, right? Well, for the Autobots and Decepticons, all that stuff is child's play compared to these...

Everyday Pet Peeves of TRANSFORMERS

Trying to look intimidating with a bunch of pizzeria flyers jammed under your windshield wipers.

Taking a snooze in the "wrong part of town"—and waking up hours later without your arms or legs.

When your hands can turn into powerful laser-cannons, there's always a chance that accidental suicide is as close as your next nose-pick.

WRITER: JACOB LAMBERT ARTIST: TOM BUNK

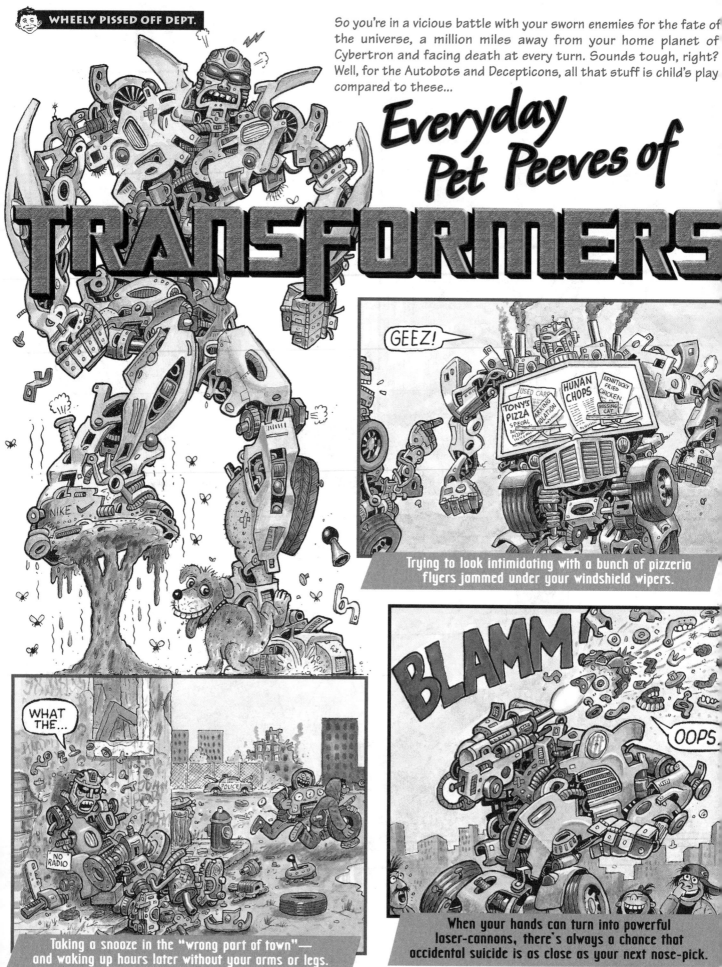

Asking the lazy gas station attendant to "do the windshield"— and then stumbling into battle with a blurry, grease-streaked visor.

Trying to find a Pep Boys anywhere that can get parts for your antimolecular photon blaster.

Finding that some jerk has stuck a Calvin sticker on your trunk when you weren't looking.

The deep, deep shame that comes every time your interplanetary loneliness leads you to cuddle with an unsuspecting VW Beetle.

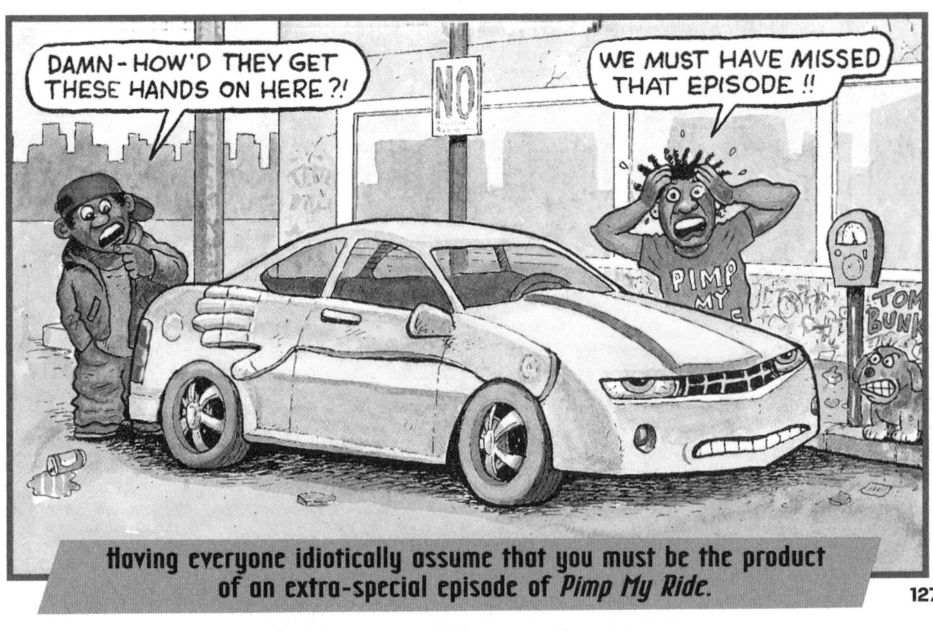

Having everyone idiotically assume that you must be the product of an extra-special episode of *Pimp My Ride*.

Sergio Aragonés presents a MAD Loo

WRITER AND ARTIST: SERGIO ARAGONÉS

at BULLIES

EATS MEETS JEST DEPT.

The MAD WORLD of...

Hello, would you like to sponsor a child?

No, I want to sign up *my* two kids!

Excuse me, we're wondering what we should order.

Tell the server you want 我希望支付那其它夫婦.

What would you like?

我希望支付那其它夫婦.

Did you te the waite what I sai

You **just ate!** ou can't **swim** for n **hour** or you'll get **cramps.**

My **teacher** told me that's a **myth** that's been **disproved.**

Listen, just because it's **not true** doesn't make it **all right!**

FOOD

WRITER: STAN SINBERG

ARTIST: MARC HEMPEL

ongratulations! w long have you een **pregnant?**

I'm **not...**

I'm **just** eating for **two...**

I **did,** ank you. od night.

Here you go. I'll take that when you're **ready.**

What? This is a **mistake!** We didn't **order** yet!

But you **just** told me, "I'd like to **pay** for that **other couple.**"

What would you like on your pizza? Sausage? Mushrooms?

The works!

What would you like on your sundae? Whipped cream? Nuts?

The works!

What would you like for your stomach? Antacid? Alka-Seltzer?

The works!

Today at school, the kids made fun of my eating disorder.

Your WHAT? You don't have an eating disorder. You eat three balanced, nutritious meals a day.

At my school, that IS an eating disorder!

DOG CATCHER

Boy, I am really out of shape. I'd do almost anything to lose weight.

Well, all you have to do is eat less.

I said ALMOST anything!

THE DWAYNE CHRONICLES

WRITER AND ARTIST: ERIC SCOTT

A couple of years ago, they made a movie called "Star Wars." It was a smash hit so they announced that they would make a sequel. Everybody thought it would be called "Star Wars II"...but, lo and behold, they called it "Episode V"! Which means that "Star Wars" was actually "Star Wars IV," and "Star Wars VI" through "X" will be made after "V" but before "I" through "III"! In any case, they'd better surpass this sequel, which doesn't compare to the original! In fact...

THE EMPIRE STRIKES OUT

BORES

Arrgg! Arrgg!
Poor Chew-bacco! Is he crying because Lube isn't back yet?
No, he's crying because this is the THIRD planet we've been on that doesn't have BANANAS growing on it!
Well, I'm going out to look for Lube!
With the temperature falling, your Wonton will freeze to death in 20 minutes!
No, he won't! This morning for breakfast, instead of his usual Chicken Soup, I gave him a bowl of ANTI-FREEZE!
SEND THIS BOY TO PLANET OF THE APES

I'm doomed! A creature captured me and I'm . . .
It's OLDIE VON MOLDIE!! Oldie . . . what are you doing UPSIDE-DOWN . . . ?!?
Lube . . .
Lube, you idiot! YOU'RE the one who's upside-down!

ARTIST: MORT DRUCKER WRITER: DICK DE BARTOLO

Lube, listen to me! You must go to the Dairybar System! There, you will learn from Yodel, the Jet-Eye Master who taught me!
Sounds great, Oldie! But first, who's going to teach me how to get down from HERE?
Your lightsaber is nearby! Whatever you WISH into your hand shall BE in your hand!
Really?? Then FORGET about the lightsaber! I'M going to wish for a sexy BLONDE with a big pair of scissors!

Lube! Thank God you're alive! I've brought you some food! But first, I must get you warm! I'm cutting open my dead Wonton and spreading his intestines and his liver and his kidneys all over you! That'll get you warm! Now about the food—
Ulp! Choke! Gagg!
Er, Ham . . . FORGET about the food! I seem to have lost my—ulp—appetite for some reason!!

I FOUND them! I FOUND Lube and Ham! And they're both fine, despite that blistering storm!
Lube used The Force to create some palm trees and sunshine!
CLUB MED

How's Lube, Doc? Did being out in that FRIGID COLD all night do any damage?
No! But some idiot covered him with animal guts! THAT did damage! But now that he's in the Hydro-Bath, he's no longer suffering from GUT EXPOSURE!
Then why does he LOOK like he's in pain?!?
Because NOW he suffering from DROWNING!!! TOO MUCH HYDR BATH! STOP TH HYDRO-BATH! R move the RUBBE HYDRO-DUCK!!

Ham, now that the emergency is over, why not get on your 90-ton broom and fly out of here?!
Oh? What makes you say that?
Princess, sometimes I think you forgot how to be a woman!
Well . . . for openers, you have your BRA on backwards!
BO DEREK I'M NOT!

C'mon, Princess! Stop pretending you dislike me! Last night, you showed your TRUE feelings for me!
As I recall, last night, I kicked you in the rear thruster!!
Yeah, but not all that hard! If that isn't love, what is?!

I'LL show you how much I love you, Ham Yoyo!!
That broad's g great lips, bu lousy eyesigh

Princess . . . we have a visitor!
It's not at the door! It's on the radar screen! See?
Tell him we gave at the other planet!
Good Lord!! It's a stainless steel COCKROACH! Those things get more indestructible each century!

I'm afraid that was an Imperial Draidle! Which means they know that we're here!
We have to vacate . . .
No! My plan is to remain here, and nothing will upset my plan!!
Oh, yeah?? How abo if I KISS you . . . ??
That MAY upset my STOMACH . . . but not my plan!!
ATARI
POW!

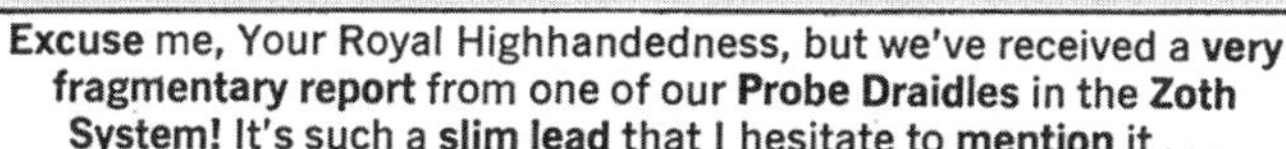

Excuse me, Your Royal Highhandedness, but we've received a **very fragmentary report** from one of our **Probe Draidles** in the **Zoth System!** It's such a **slim lead** that I hesitate to **mention** it . . .
That's it! That's **EXACTLY** where **Lube Skystalker,** the **Princess** and the **rebels ARE!**
But out of **ten million places** to **hide** in the universe, **why THERE?**
Why NOT . . . ?!?
Good Lord, your **Imperial Logic** is **overwhelming!** We shall **attack** Zoth **at once!**
REPORT

Princess Laidup, **six Star Destroyers** are on their way here . . .
We'll **open** the **Energy Shield** for a **moment** to let the **Fighters** out . . . !
Fighters against **Imperial Star Destroy-ers . . . ?!**
Don't worry! I'll make sure you're **covered** by our **Ion Cannon . . .** and by our **Major Medical Policy!**

These **Imperial Klunkers** have **armor so thick,** our lasers **bounce off them!** Which is **why** I'm making a pass across this one's **legs** with a **clothesline!**
WHOOSH

It **worked!!** It **worked!** Did the clothesline **tangle up** the Klunker's **legs** and **TRIP it?**
No, the clothesline had all our **Yucchies' dirty laundry** on it! When the Klunker puts **its leg up to its nose** to **block the smell,** it **FELL OVER!!**

We've been **HIT! Hold on tight!!** I'll **try** to find a **CLEARING** to **crash-land** into!

A **CLEARING?!?** This planet has a **million square miles of flat ice . . .** and **he's** going to look for a **clearing!**

I may have crash-landed my **Fighter,** but I'm **still** going to try to destroy another one of those **Imperial Klunkers!!**
WHOOSH

Take THAT!!
Hee-Hee-Hoo-Hoo-Hah-Hah!!

You've **got** to know **exactly** where to **TICKLE** those silly things!!

KA BLOOM!

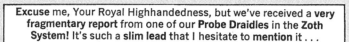

Hold on, Princess! It's time to leave!
Hah!! Do you really think this bucket of bolts will get us OUT of here?!?
Hey, this is the Aluminum Falcon! This baby's still got a lot of surprises left in her!!
Sir! The entire control panel just shorted out!
See? There's ONE SURPRISE already! And there should be plenty more!!

Well, Princess, I DID manage to get us out of one very tight jam . . .
Look! We're entering an ASTEROID BELT!!
And into another very tight jam! Creepio . . . what do you recommend for ASTEROIDS?
May I suggest you try Preparation H?
Mets

Well, Bar-Stool! Here we are on the planet Dairybar!
Oh, I'm sure it's perfectly safe for Draidles! What I'm worried about is: Is it safe for HUMANS?! But after seeing snow and ice for so long, it's nice to have a change of scene . . . Slime, muck, quicksand, snakes, bats, mist . . .
Bleep Blap Boop Beeep
Beep Bapp Boop! Bleep Screeeep!
Yeah . . . I'M beginning to miss the snow and ice, too!

Welcome to Dairybar! May I help you?
Why . . . yes! I'm looking for a great warrior and Jet-Eye Master named Yodel! I KNOW it seems strange to be looking for a person like that in a slimy mudhole like this, but—
SLIMY MUDHOLE?!? This is my HOME!
Well, I don't exactly consider YOU to be MR. CLEAN!

I am Yodel! I can teach you everything! How to levitate objects, how to fight with a lightsaber, how to transmute metals, how to catch flies on your tongue! I also give an advanced course in "Cute"!
Good! Let's get started!
The FIRST thing you must learn is patience!
Don't talk to me about patience! I've got tons of patience! Now—let's get going, you slimy twit!!
MISS PIGGY FAN CLUB

There's something STRANGE about this asteroid cave we've landed in!
Y-Y-You mean the way the rocks are shaped? That one looks like a giant liver . . . and that one looks like a giant stomach . . .
The one that worries ME is the one that looks like a giant HEART . . . mainly because it's BEATING!
Let's get out of here!

Holy cow! Will you look at that . . . ?! Is this "Star Wars V" or "Jaws III"?!

Well, Princess . . . I sure got us out of tight spot number two with no trouble!
Imperial Starship dead ahead, Sir!
And right into tight spot number THREE!!

There's the Aluminum Falcon! He's driving directly at us, head on! He must be crazy!
That, or he's got No-Fault Insurance!

xcuse me, your Royal
rdhat, but the Falcon
s totally disappeared!
feel so bad about los-
ng it, I could just die!
Your wish shall be granted!

GHACCKK!!

Chewbacco, covering the top of the Falcon with KRAZY GLUE was a stroke of genius!!
Now that we're stuck here, how are we going to get away again?
They have to dump their garbage before they can go into lightspeed!
Fantastic! This ship LOOKS like garbage, so they'll never notice us!

You've learned well, Lube! I have taught you how to lift objects like rocks and plants and heavy cases! You may be a Jet-Eye, yet!
Can you teach me how to lift wallets and watches?
Then again, maybe all is lost!
GET OFF MY CASE
PET ROCK
ROCK GROUP

Wait a minute! I'm seeing a vision of my friends! They are being betrayed! I must GO to them!
Ah! You have been given the gift of clairvoyance! What are you seeing now?
I'm seeing an Operator, from Galactic Bell, asking for $40 for the next three minutes!
I wondered how long it would take the Telephone Company to find a way to charge for ESP!

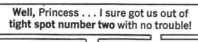

That's the planet Bedpan! They KNOW me, so we can hide there!
W-Why are they shooting at us?
Like I said.. they KNOW me!

I am Landough, The Handsome! And you—you are truly beautiful!!
Well, thank you! That's always nice to hear...!
I was TALKING to the BROAD!

Are you having problems with your Draidle...?
Er... no! He just woke up, and he's having trouble pulling himself together! However, when he TALKS, it all comes out gobbledygook!
Someone must have fitted it with a voice box for a Politician! They are EASY to fix!
MOST Politicians ARE!!

Sorry, Ham! I had to make a deal to keep the Imperial Forces off my back!
You invited Dart Zadar to dinner?!
Don't be so shocked! I know he doesn't eat out much! But for you he made an exception!

I plan on deep-freezing Lube Skystalker the moment he arrives on Bedpan in a vain attempt to rescue you! Meanwhile, I will freeze Ham Solo as a test...! Lower him into the chamber...!
Well, Ham... this looks like the end! I LOVE you!
So do I!
He SAID it! He SAID it! He LOVES ME!
No, I meant I love ME, too!

The freezing process has taken place! Did Ham Yoyo survive?
Gee, I really don't think so! He looks like Creamed Spinach!!
Excuse me, my Lord! That IS Creamed Spinach!
Ham Yoyo is in the other container... and he DID survive!
So he'll be around for "Star Wars VI" at least!

So, Lube Skystalker, you've come here in a stupid attempt to save your friends! Well, your destiny lies with ME...!!
Never!
I will give you wealth... power... spaceships... a galaxy all your own...
You're wasting your breath!!
... and beautiful girls...
How MANY beautiful girls?!?

. . . AND SO ENDS EPISODE V OF "STAR BORES"!

★★★★★★

WHEN LANDOUGH AND CHEWBACCO FIND THE FROZEN HAM YOYO, WILL HE CONTINUE TO GIVE PRINCESS LAIDUP THE COLD SHOULDER?

★★★★★★

WILL CREEPIO KEEP BABBLING ON ENDLESSLY, AND FINALLY BE ELECTED TO PUBLIC OFFICE?

★★★★★★

WILL DART ZADER STOP BEING "MR. NICE GUY," AND REALLY TRY TO DESTROY LUBE SKYSTALKER?

★★★★★★

WILL ANY OF US REALLY CARE WHAT HAPPENS, AFTER ANOTHER TWO-YEAR INTERMISSION . . . ??

History's Most Famous BOOGERS

ROMAN EMPEROR JULIUS SNEEZER

FILMMAKER GEORGE MUCUS

INDIAN PRINCESS PICK-AHONTAS

PRESIDENT TEDDY NOSE-EV

To create a masterpiece, you must **dig deep**!

PAINTER PABLO PICK-CASSO

SCIENTIST ALBERT EIN-SLIME

SINGER ICK JAGGER

EXPLORER CRUST-OPHER COLUMBUS

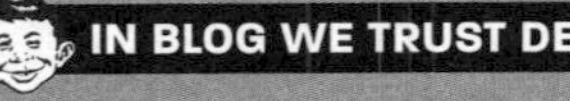

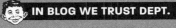

Planet TAD!!!!!

http://www.galaxyo'blogs.com/planettad

Search

Planet TAD!!!!!

[**entries**|archive|friends]

[**userinfo**|galaxyo'blogs userinfo]
[**calendar**|galaxyo'blogs calendar]

[13 September|**3:08pm**]

Hello, everyone! My name is Tad. I am fourteen years old and a freshman at Lakeville Junior High School. (Go Pirates!) (Our school mascot is the Pirate.) (I think because of the "LAKEville.") (Although, come to think of it, you find pirates in the ocean, not on lakes. Our mascot's, like, some kind of a lake pirate.) (The more I think about it, the more I realize that our mascot sucks.)

This is my new blog, which I am starting today. I've decided to start a blog because I have a lot of important thoughts to share with the world, and also to try and get Natalie Portman to go out with me.

I'm just kidding about that last part. Although if you are Natalie Portman, and you're reading this — like, if you Googled yourself or something — hi.

[14 September|**05:17pm**]

[**mood**|pissed]

I can't concentrate. My little sister Sophie is in her room, practicing for her oboe recital tomorrow night. She's been playing the same five-minute song, over and over, for the last hour, and it's not even a good song.

Although on second thought, I don't think there is such a thing as a good oboe song.

[15 September|**04:56pm**]

My friend Evan let me borrow his dad's copy of Photoshop, and I've been playing around with it on my computer. This is what Sophie would look like if she had the head

I call her Sophie Rex.

[16 September|**07:42pm**]

Evan and I spent most of lunch today debating who would win in a wrestling match: Lara Croft or the woman with the lips from the "Resident Evil" movies. (I say Lara, he says "Resident Evil" lip-lady.) We didn't resolve it, but we did agree that it's a fight we'd really like to see.

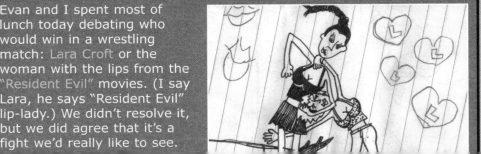

I saw a preview of King Kong on TV last night. I think if I were a giant ape trying to escape from people in airplanes trying to kill me, maybe I wouldn't climb to the top of the city's highest skyscraper. Duh!

[19 September|**03:01pm**]

[**mood**|pissed]

I can't stand Doug Spivak. He tried tripping me today. He calls me "Tard," which I guess is a play on my name. It would hurt my feelings that he's making fun of my intelligence, but Doug's the guy who read half of "Watership Down" for English class before he realized it was about rabbits.

[20 September|**03:19pm**]

[**mood**|pissed]

Bad news. Mom found a printout of Sophie Rex. She and Dad say I'm not allowed to use Photoshop on pictures of Sophie anymore. But she didn't say anything about pictures of THEM.

This is what my parents looked like when they were newly married, and if they had chipmunk heads.

[21 September|**05:31pm**]

In English today, Mr. Carlson had us spend the whole class diagramming sentences at the blackboard. Diagramming sentences is like a combination of the worst parts of doing math with the worst parts of doing English. It's a total waste of time, because you can either speak English or you can't, and if you can't there's no point in drawing lines all over your sentences. Doug Spivak thinks that "gooder" means the same thing as "better" and no amount of diagramming sentences will fix that.

Besides, it's a waste of time. I asked Dad at dinner whether there's any job where you have to diagram sentences, and he said, "Teaching junior high kids English."

Mr. Carlson hard at work.

[22 September|**07:47pm**]

Today Mr. Carlson had us diagram sentences again. I told him that I didn't want to have to keep doing this, because the only job where you have to diagram sentences is junior high teacher, and I planned on doing something better than that. He didn't say anything, he just got very quiet and gave us all a pop quiz on diagramming sentences. I got a D. Doug Spivak blamed me for the pop quiz, and he told me to meet him behind the gym after school so he could kick my butt. I decided not to go.

WRITER: TIM CARVELL **ARTIST: BRIAN DURNIAK**

JOKE AND DAGGER DEPT.

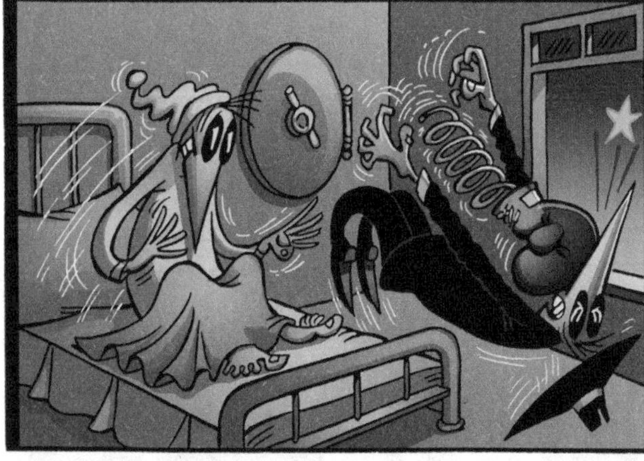

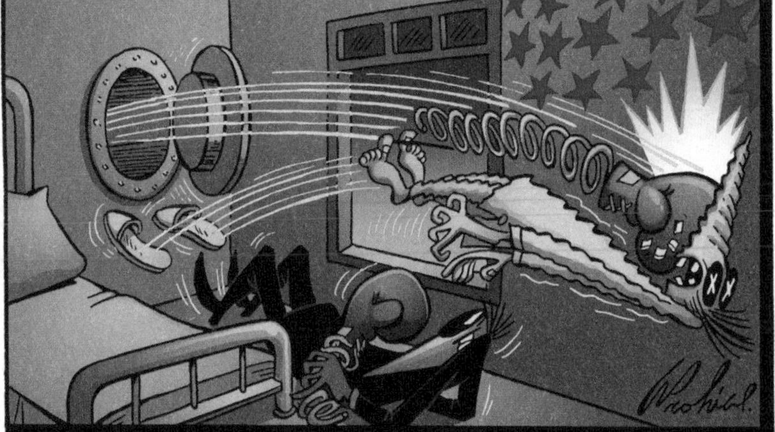

WRITER AND ARTIST: ANTONIO PROHIAS COLORIST: CARRIE STRACHAN

F LEMONY SNICKET WROTE ABOUT THE SERIES OF UNFORTUNATE EVENTS IN YOUR LIFE

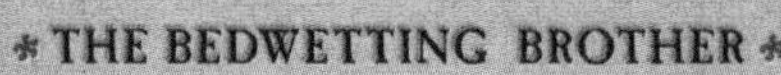

Your Series of Unfortunate Events
HELP
SCHOOL BUS
KEEP BACK 50 FEET
Book the Dth
by LEMONY SNICKET
THE DEMENTED DRIVER

ARTIST: GARY HALLGREN

Your Series of Unfortunate Events
Book the Eth
by LEMONY SNICKET
THE EVIL EGGING
Your Series of Unfortunate Events
Book the Fth
by LEMONY SNICKET
THE FATAL FISHTANK
Your Series of Unfortunate Events
Book the Gth
by LEMONY SNICKET
THE GASSY GRANDPARENTS
Your Series of Unfortunate Events
SOLVE BY MON.
READ 140 PP IN GEO TEXT.
DO ALL 50 PROBLEMS
Book the Hth
by LEMONY SNICKET
THE HORRIFIC HOMEWORK
Your Series of Unfortunate Events
Book the Ith
by LEMONY SNICKET
THE INESCAPABLE IMMUNIZATION
Your Series of Unfortunate Events
Book the Jth
by LEMONY SNICKET
THE JUVENILE JAMMIES
Your Series of Unfortunate Events
Book the Kth
by LEMONY SNICKET
THE KILLER KARATE CLASS
Your Series of Unfortunate Events
Book the Lth
by LEMONY SNICKET
THE LOUSY LUNCH

Your Series of Unfortunate Events

Book the Mth by LEMONY SNICKET

THE MEDDLING MOTHER

Your Series of Unfortunate Events

Book the Nth by LEMONY SNICKET

THE NASTY NECKTIE

Your Series of Unfortunate Events

Book the Oth by LEMONY SNICKET

THE OBNOXIOUS ORNAMENT

Your Series of Unfortunate Events

Book the Pth by LEMONY SNICKET

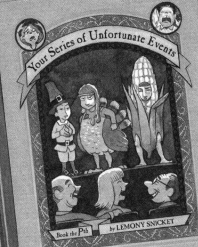

THE PATHETIC PAGEANT

Your Series of Unfortunate Events

Book the Qth by LEMONY SNICKET

THE QUEASY QUIZ

Your Series of Unfortunate Events

Book the Rth by LEMONY SNICKET

THE RAINY RECESS

Your Series of Unfortunate Events

Book the Sth by LEMONY SNICKET

THE SWELTERING SUMMER SCHOOL

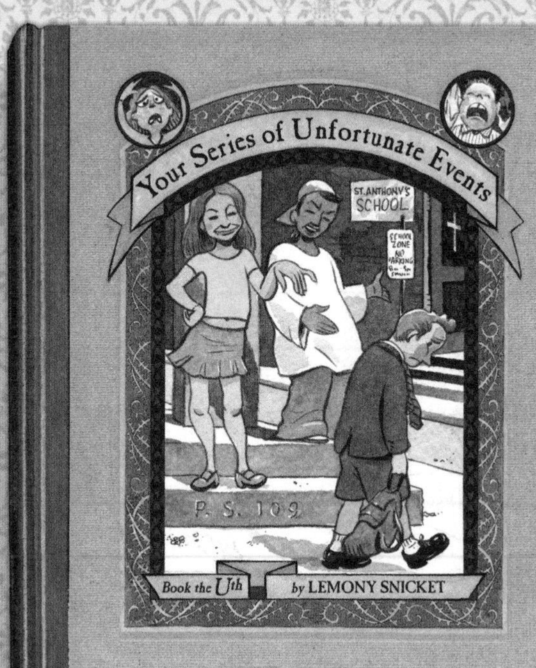
Your Series of Unfortunate Events
ST. ANTHONY'S SCHOOL
P. S. 109
Book the Uth
by LEMONY SNICKET
THE UNFASHIONABLE UNIFORM

Your Series of Unfortunate Events
Book the Vth
by LEMONY SNICKET
THE VILE VEGETABLES

Your Series of Unfortunate Events
Book the Wth
by LEMONY SNICKET
THE WICKED WEDGIE

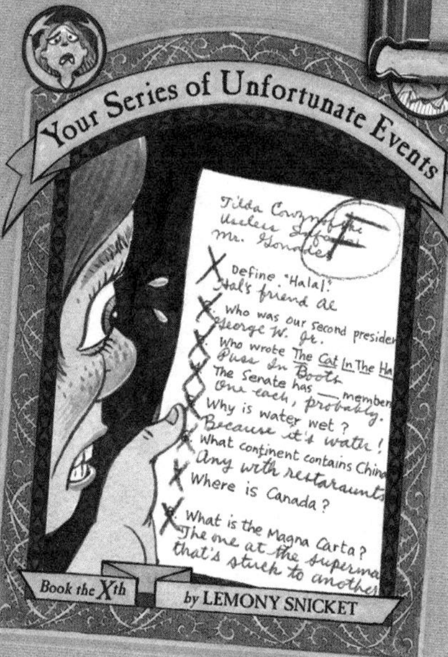
Your Series of Unfortunate Events
Book the Xth
by LEMONY SNICKET
THE EXCESSIVE X'S

Your Series of Unfortunate Events
COMICS
Book the Yth
by LEMONY SNICKET
THE YUCKY YARD SALE

Your Series of Unfortunate Events
ZIPPP
Book the Zth
by LEMONY SNICKET
THE ZEALOUS ZIPPERER

ANOTHER MORNING ON FIFTH AVENUE

ARTIST: PAUL COKER WRITER: DUCK EDWING

SONGS for PEOPLE

(ALL SONGS MAY BE SUNG TO THE TUNE OF THE SPONGEBOB SQUAREPANTS THEM

THE LUNCH LADY

Who's dishing up food that's
disgustingly gross?
The Lunch Lady!
Is anything edible? Not even close!
The Lunch Lady!

If you're feeling brave give
the chili a try!
The Lunch Lady!
That is if you think
it's your day to die!

Ready!

Her big lunch treat!
Is some brown meat!
Smells like bad feet!
We say – don't eat!

OUR MATH TEACHER

Whose class is so boring it puts us to sleep?
Our Math Teacher!
Gives homework so tough that we go home and w
Our Math Teacher!

He dreams about fractions, thinks angles are neat
Our Math Teacher!
Likes to convert things from inches to feet!
Our Math Teacher!

Ready!

We hate his class!
It's like bad gas!
He's a jackass!
No way – we'll pass!

n YOUR SCHOOL

THE CLASS BULLY

Who's big and who's scary and
  mean as can be?
The Class Bully!
He beats you up daily at twenty to three!
The Class Bully!

When you see him coming it's
  best just to run!
The Class Bully!
A wedgie for you is his kind of fun!

Ready!

All brawn, no brain!
Loves to give pain!
He can't refrain!
He's just – insane!

WRITER: ANDREW J. SCHWARTZBERG ARTIST: TOM RICHMOND

SCHOOL BUS DRIVER

Who drives on the sidewalk and
  blows through red lights?
School Bus Driver!
His hearing is going and his vision bites!
School Bus Driver!

We wonder how he got his license at all!
School Bus Driver!
We think it's a fake he bought at the mall!

Ready!

Our bones will break!
In fear we quake!
Please sir, please brake!
A cab – we'll take!

WORDS TO GLIB BY DEPT.

Parents, teachers and other authority figures have a miraculous gif
shutting off any topic of conversation they don't wish to pursue. T
just come out of left field with some obscure, presumably wise old sa

MAD PROVERBS GUARANTEE

WRITER: TOM

axiom which you don't understand. But now you can have the power to nce THEIR boring, insipid and unwanted talk, simply by memorizing this y collection of deeply philosophical, but absolutely meaningless...

O LEAVE 'EM SPEECHLESS

ST: AL JAFFEE

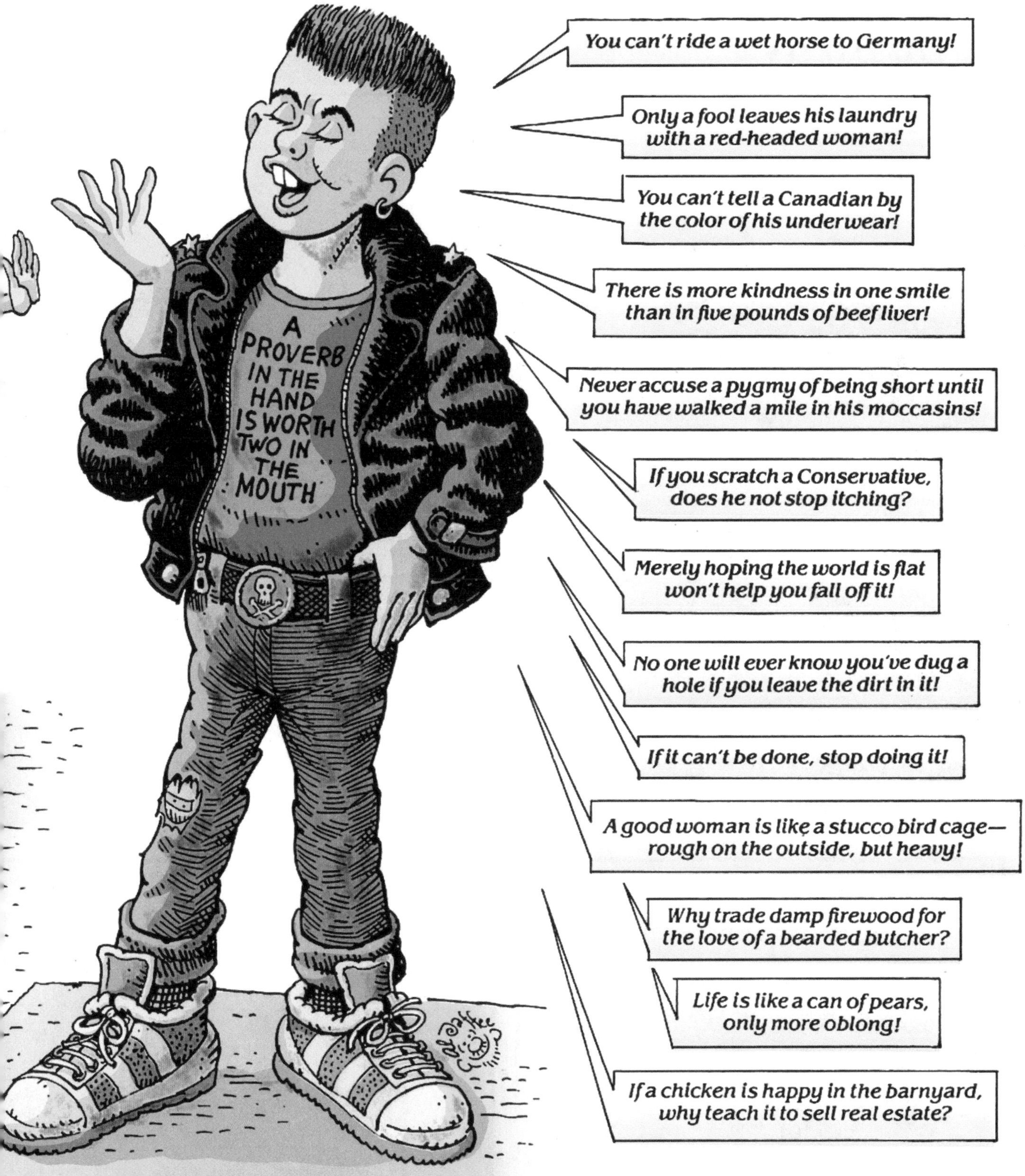

DON MARTIN DEPT.

ONE FINE DAY DURING LUNCH PERIOD

WRITER AND ARTIST: DON MARTIN

Cents-Less Coupons

R MONEY-SAVING CIRCULAR

DENTA-FROST

Toothpaste & Cake Frosting

NEW!

So Sweet it Hurts Your Teeth—While CLEANING Them!*

*Clinically proven to fight cavities while causing them. (ADA Report, 3/2002)

TRY ALL FIVE ANTISEPTIC VARIETIES!

NEW! DENTA-FROST
Toothpaste & Cake Frosting
Plaque-Fighting Coconut Pecan
NET WT. 12 OZ (340g)

A MAD FAKEOUT AD

NEW! DENTA-FROST
Toothpaste & Cake Frosting
Chocolate Fudge with Whitening Power™
NET WT. 12 OZ (340g)

NEW! DENTA-FROST
Toothpaste & Cake Frosting
Tartar-Control Cream Cheese Supreme™
NET WT. 12 OZ (340g)

NEW! DENTA-FROST
Toothpaste & Cake Frosting
Sparkling Milk Chocolate
NET WT. 12 OZ (340g)

MANUFACTURER'S COUPON
NOT VALID IN AMERICA

SAVE 25¢

when you buy any flavor
DENTA-FROST
Toothpaste & Cake Frosting

Consumer: If you try to use this coupon in a supermarket, the cashier will not only start laughing and pointing, but will call over the other cashiers, who will also start laughing and pointing, and all the shoppers waiting on line will get angry at you. It's true!

Somedays you just don't have time to shoot, fetch and skin a mess of squirrels for vittles.

And who can afford fresh squirrel at supermarket prices? Inbred Valley to the rescue!

SKWIRL™ Imitation Squirrel Meat tastes just like the real thing. Affordable, too! And we reckon that furry little guy in the oak tree just might thank you.

MANUFACTURER'S COUPON
EXPIRES APRIL 30, 1971

Save 75¢

When you purchase ONE 6 ounce package of Inbred Valley SKWIRL™ Imitation Squirrel Meat

Consumer: Lose weight now, ask me how! I lost 40 pounds in 2 months! You can too! No dieting, exercise, etc. Call 800-555-5728 for details. 24 hr. recorded message.

SKWIRL™

Qwik & Easy Skwirl™-Loaf

1 package (6 oz.)
SKWIRL™ Imitation Squirrel Meat
1 cup catsup
2 handfuls bread, mooshed-up*

1. **Dump all 'gredients in a pot.**
2. **Scrunch into a loafy shape.**
3. **Put in oven.**
4. **Bake until cooked.**

Serves 2 to 14 pendin' on how many mouths need feedin'.

***sawdust may be substituted**

"I used to have to threaten to put the cat to sleep before the kids would clean the litter box. Now they can't wait to do it!"

NEW!

FUNCLUMPS™

SHAPE-CLUMPING CAT LITTER

Eliminates Odor!
Reduces Tracking!
Clumps Urine Into Fun Shapes!

MFR COUPON EXPIRES NOW

FUNCLUMPS™

$1 OFF

Shape-Clumping Cat Litter

Consumer: Call us up and let us know when and where you're going to try and use this coupon. We want to see you explain to the store manager why you're trying to redeem a coupon for a product that does not exist. On second thought, don't call us. We know how you'll sound: very, very stupid!

A MAD FAKEOUT AD

Sergio Aragonés Presents a MAD look

PAINTBALL

FLAG

FLAG

PAINT BALL

FLAG

SPLATT!
FLAG

PAINT BALL

URBAN QUEST
PAINTBALL PLAYING FIELD
OXNARD CA.
BARREL PLUGS IN

GRRR!

SPLAT!

ART GALLERY

G*!!★@!
Grrr
OJAI SURPLUS!

SPLATT!
SPLATT!

SPLAT!

G*!!*

? ?

SPLATT!

THAWP! THAWP!
THAP! THAP!

G*!!
ARAGONÉS 05

JOKE AND DAGGER DEPT.

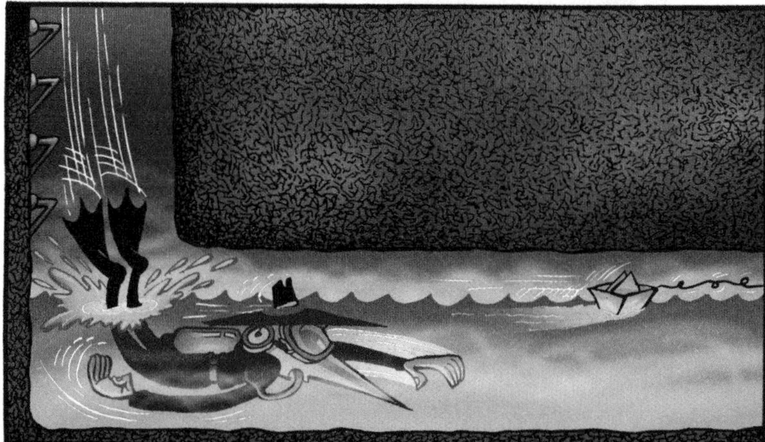

WRITER AND ARTIST: ANTONIO PROHIAS COLORIST: CARRIE STRACHAN

GEEK TRAGEDIES DEPT.

Aiiieeeee! Hide the kids! Batten down the hatches! Run for your lives! They're back! Here come the dorks, morons and nerds whose yellow teeth and zit-covered faces fill the rogues' gallery of dweebs we call MAD's...

Video Arcade Personalities

VOLUME II

ARTIST: TOM BUNK
WRITER: SEAN EISENPORTH

THE REFLECTOR

The one thing that arcade players fear most is the dreaded Reflector in their video game screens. Hovering close, staring over their shoulders like some anal-retentive math teacher, this clueless turd is completely unaware of his highly annoying and intrusive presence!

Video Arcade Personalities

THE COAT-HANGER

Beware The Coat-Hanger! This big gooch deliberately hangs his jacket on the joystick of the game next to him hoping that someone will ask him to remove it. The instant the request is made, The Coat-Hanger takes it as his cue to perform radical dental alterations with his steel-toe boots on the poor schmuck who asked him!

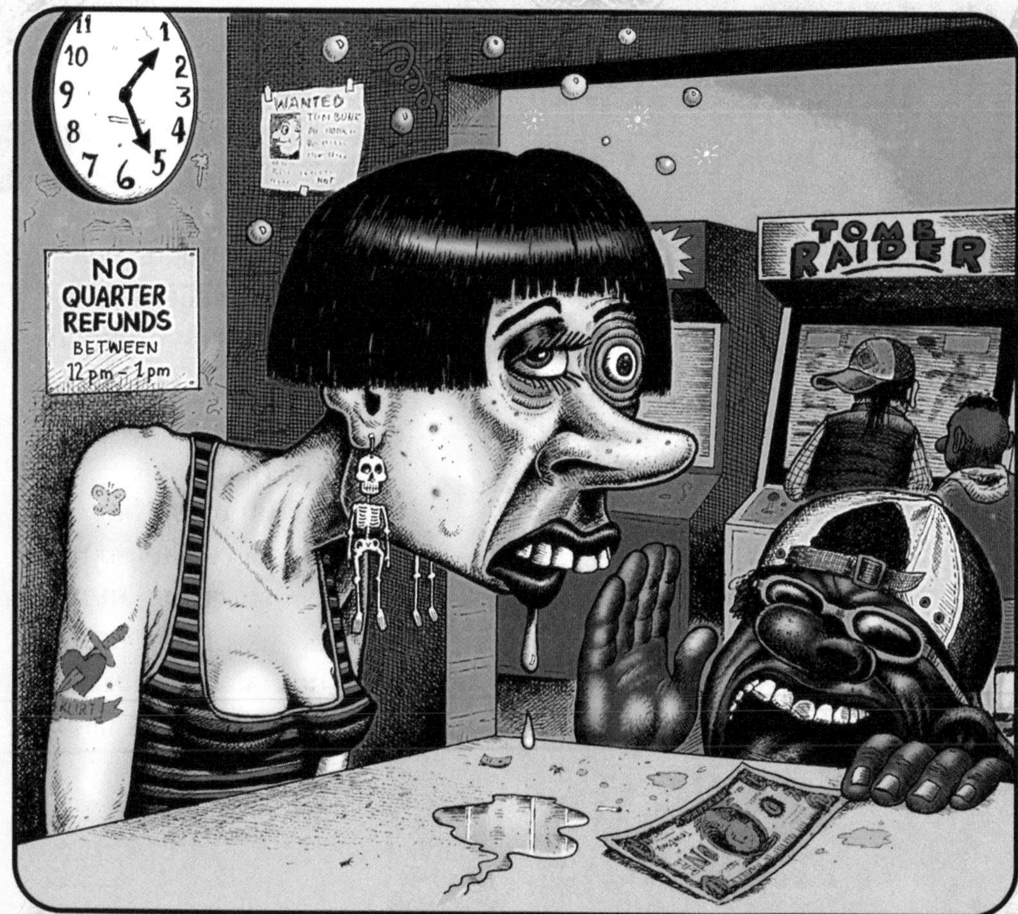

THE LIVING DE

She's got no pulse! She's got about as much brain wave activity as a Twinkie! She is The Living Dead! Hey, you'd turn into a mindless, drooling zombie too if the entire purpose of your failed and bleak life was to hand out change all day to a perpetual parade of illiterate, unwashed freaks!

THE CURSOR

You can't always see The Cursor, but you can always hear him! This profane pinhead feels compelled to make his fury known to everyone in the arcade! And the comedic irony of it all is that no matter how much he is enraged by any one particular game, he continues to plop quarters into it! Sheesh! Talk about your pathetic codependent relationships!

KILLING TIME
NO NO NO! Ya hafta hit the "kick" and "defense" buttons at the same time, then go ←↑↓↑←↑←↑↓↑←↑ to do the INVERTED CARTWHEEL ROUND-HOUSE POWER KICK OF DEATH!!

THE ADVISOR

The Advisor runs around the arcade spewing his unsolicited advice to many a captive audience. This well-meaning but utterly misguided cretin has made it his life's mission to correct any and all game-playing errors he sees. He has to somehow occupy his time — ever since the editors of the video game magazines stopped printing his obnoxious letters!

Good news! Zombies are making a comeback! It used to be that these creatures were feared and despised by the general populatio[n] but no more! Still, don't pop those champagne corks for zombies just yet! Being a zombie ain't easy, as you'll see in...

JOHN CALDWELL'S

THINGS THAT REALLY GET UNDER A ZOMBIE'S SKIN

WRITER AND ARTIST: JOHN CALDWELL

The fact that, no matter how hard he tries, he's never among the first 100 patrons to get something for free

When, just before a big date, his face breaks out in nightcrawlers

Picnic ants

Flip-flopping government studies saying one day that eating brains lowers cholesterol, then the next day, declaring just the opposite

Getting Punk'd

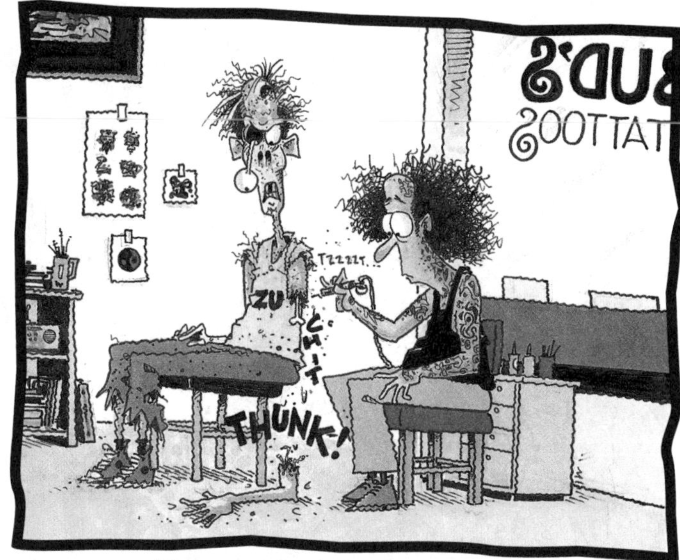

The seemingly insurmountable problems associated with getting a barbed wire bicep tattoo

The time it takes to find a limb that fell off while you were sleeping

Seriously mis-timing that hand-popping-out-from-the-grave moment

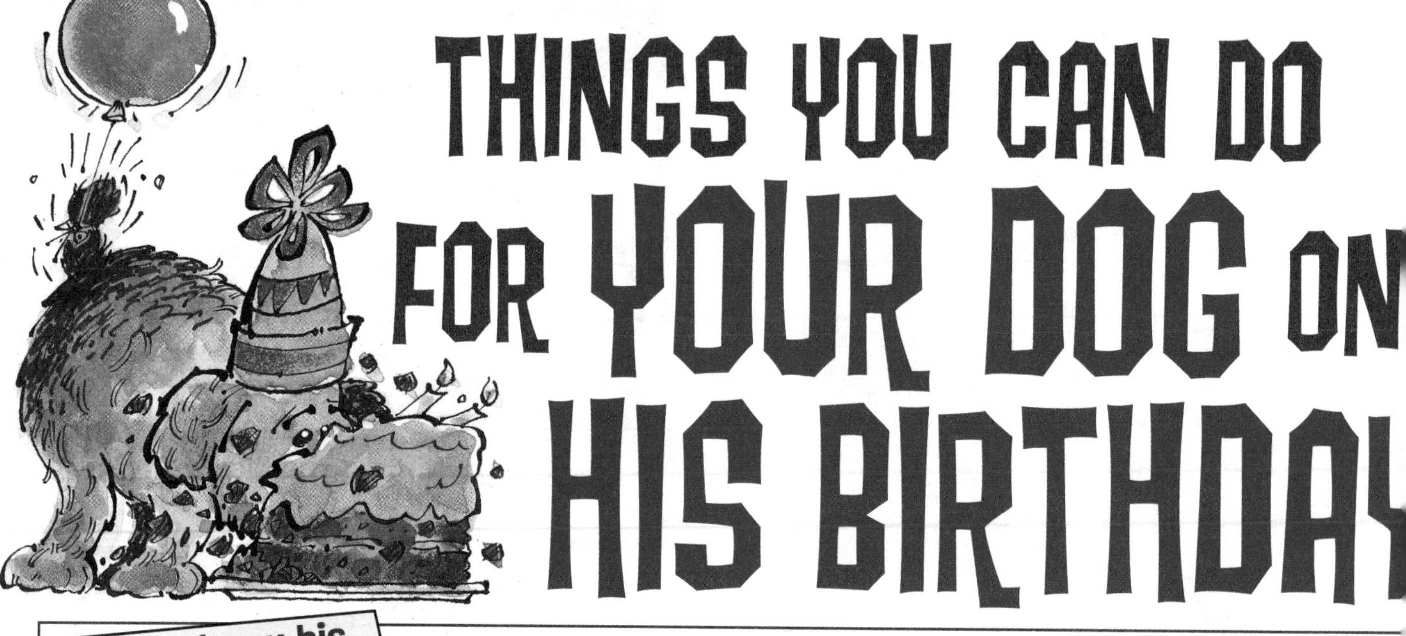
THINGS YOU CAN DO
FOR YOUR DOG ON
HIS BIRTHDAY

Let him throw his very own party!

Perform a trick for him!
Play "Happy Birthday" on a high-pitched dog whistle!

Share his hobby with him!

Help him dig holes in your neighbor's lawn!

Give him the use of your bed for the day!
Jayhawk

Let him eat first and you get HIS table scraps!

WRITER: PAUL PETER PORGES ARTIST: PAUL COKER

Walk him the very moment he wants you to!

Have a drink with him at his private fountain!

Collect several weeks of garbage for him to go through!

Dress up as a mailman and let him chase you!

THE CONTINUING ADVENTURES OF WILLY NILLY

WRITER: MO WILLEMS ARTIST: JACOB CHABOT

Just pick a different item from each row
as you read your way down the page and you'll have
a ridiculous new SpongeBob episode every time!
MAKE YOUR OWN SCREWY SPONGEBOB SQUAREPANTS EPISODE
WRITER: KENT PARKER
ARTIST: STEVE SMALLWOOD
WHEN
SPONGEBOB
PATRICK
MR. KRABS
GARY
BARNACLE BOY
SQUIDWARD
LARRY THE LOBSTER
PLANKTON
GOES TO VISIT
SANDY'S TREEDOME
THE BATHROOM
URANUS
YOUR GRANDMOTHER
GOKU
TOKYO DISNEY
THE DENTIST
FOSTER'S HOME FOR IMAGINARY FRIENDS
HE IS SHOCKED TO FIND AN OUT OF CONTROL
FLYING DUTCHMAN
NINTENDOG
BRATZ DOLL
ARTHUR
J.K. ROWLING
TOILET
GERBIL
DINOSAUR SKELETON

MERMAIDMAN
LONG DIVISION
THE OLSEN TWINS
A PICKLE JAR
ELMO
A RUNNY NOSE
THE CHICKENPOX
AN ITCHY SWEATER
AND THREATENING THE WORLD WITH
POISONOUS SEA URCHINS
TARTAR SAUCE
DIARRHEA
SUMMER SCHOOL
TOENAIL FUNGUS
A SPANKING
"CAN YOU HEAR ME NOW?" COMMERCIALS
CLONE TROOPERS
BUT WITH THE HELP OF
PAINTY THE PIRATE
ADAM SANDLER
KIM POSSIBLE
KING KONG
MARIO
DRAKE AND JOSH
THE GHOST OF ELVIS
THE FORCE
EVERYONE GOES ON A SCAVENGER HUNT WHERE THE PRIZE IS
THE SECRET KRABBY PATTY RECIPE
LUNCH WITH QUEEN LATIFAH
CLEAN UNDERWEAR
PEACE ON EARTH
HARRY POTTER'S WAND
ACCORDION LESSONS
AN XBOX 360
A METALLIC OUTER SHELL
AND THEY ALL END UP LIVING
IN A PINEAPPLE UNDER THE SEA
IN MINNESOTA
IN OUTER SPACE
AT TITANS TOWER
NEXT DOOR TO YOU
TO REGRET IT
IN AN IGLOO
IN THE WHITE HOUSE

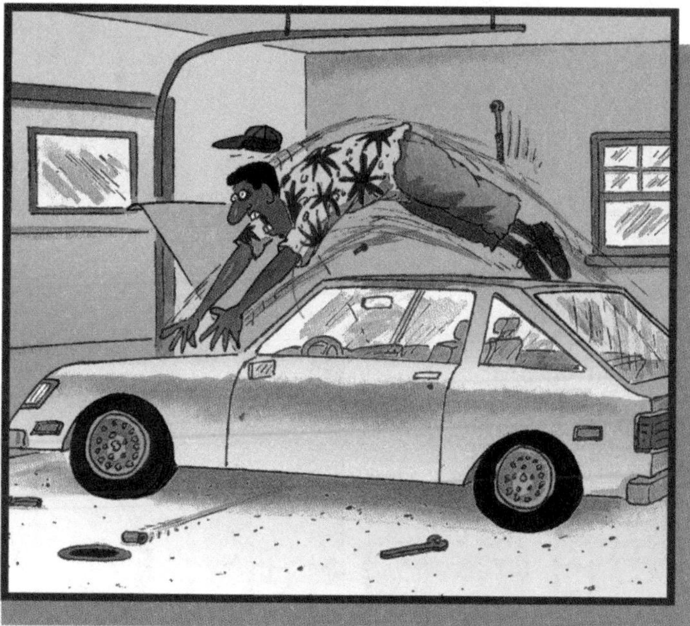

The **more** you paid for a socket wrench, the **faster** it will roll towards the garage floor drain when dropped.

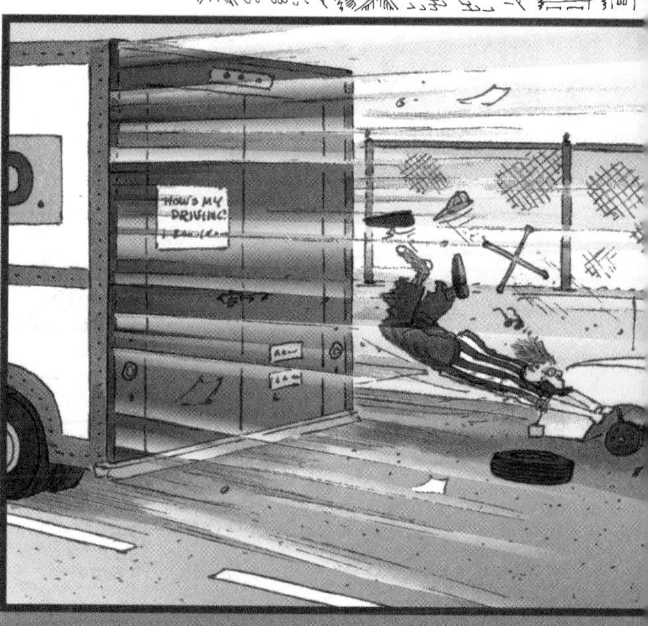

A tire that goes flat on a high-speed expressway will **always** b
located on the driver's side of the car.

AS A PUBLIC SERVICE, MAD IS OFFERING SOME TIPS FOR ALL YOU AU
ENTHUSIASTS WHO LIKE TO PUT ON YOUR COVERALLS, GET UNDER THE HO

THE CAST IRON LA

WRITER AND ARTIST: TOM CHENEY

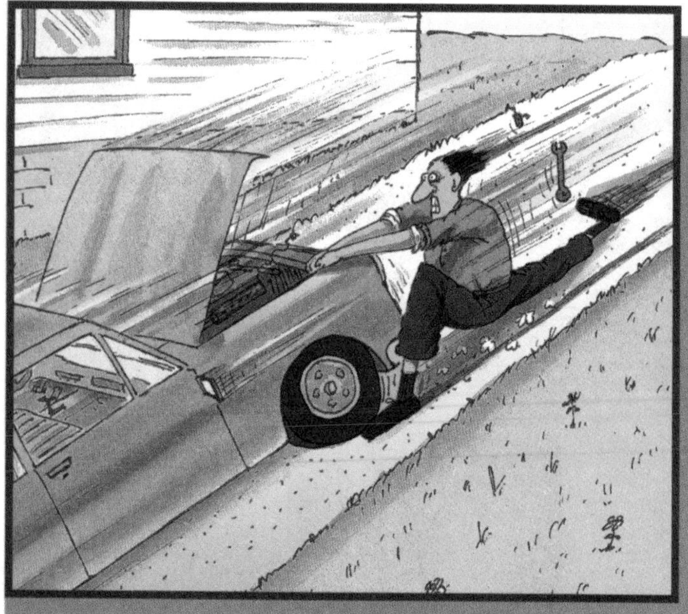

Virtually **any** part you remove from a car parked on a sloped driveway will be directly connected to the emergency brake system.

An airbag that fails to inflate during a collision will **always** inf
when you attempt to carry it back to the auto parts store in your p

A part that can only be adjusted while the engine is running will **always** be located one inch or less from a spinning fan belt.

A horn that never works will **refuse** to shut itself off if you attempt to repair it after 2:00 a.m.

AND GIVE IT THE OL' LUBE JOB...AND PEOPLE WHO LIKE TO FIX CARS, TOO! SO, F YOU WANT TO ADD NEW 'SPARK TO THOSE PLUGS, MAKE SURE YOU KNOW...

VS OF CAR REPAIR

When you traveled to England last month you decided to pull out all the stops and go first class — so you had beef for dinner every night...Aren't *you* the genius!

e least expensive and most frequently replaced part on your car can **never** be reached without first removing the entire engine.

A grease gun will never accidentally discharge, **unless** it's pointed at an open car window.

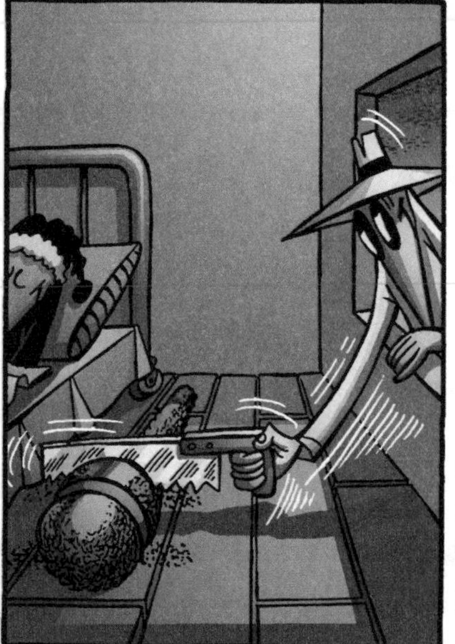

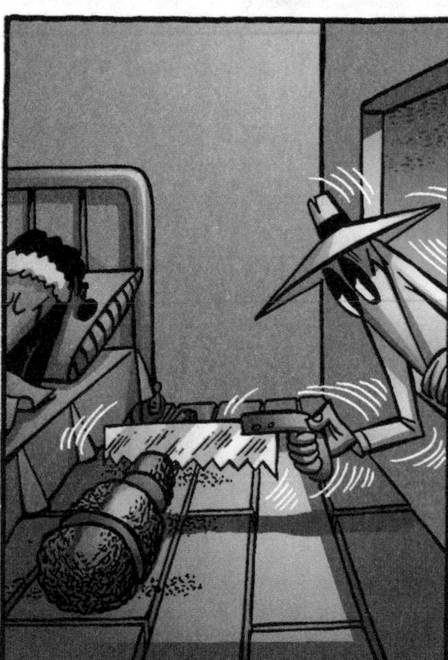

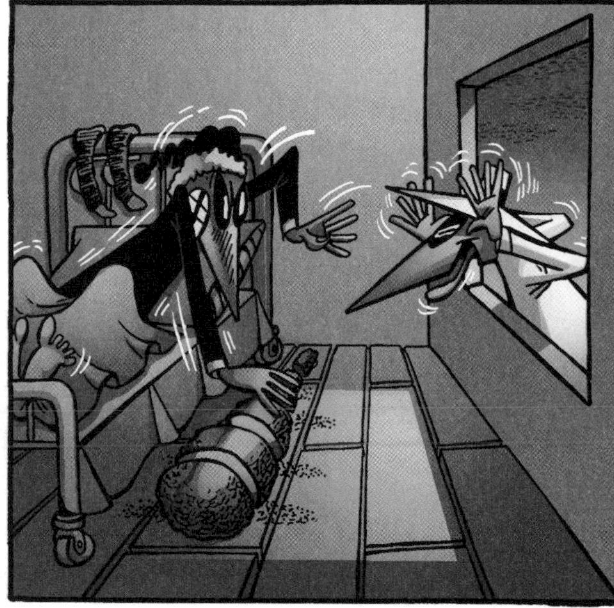

WRITER AND ARTIST: ANTONIO PROHIAS COLORIST: CARRIE STRACHAN

There are some wonderful books that have been around for 40 years and are loved by all. The following isn't one of them! Hold your nose, it's...

THE BIG POT OF BEANS

Mr. And Mrs. Rumproast were just getting home from their jobs when their younger son, Arthur, called from the bedroom he shared with his brother, Stanley.

"Hey! Come and look! Hey!"

Mr. And Mrs. Rumproast rushed to the bedroom and saw Stanley lying on his bed.

"Is he sick?" asked Mrs. Rumproast.

"Give it a few seconds," answered Arthur.

And indeed, in just five seconds, the room was filled with a loud "Poooot!" sound and Stanley raised four feet above his bed. Then, Mr. and Mrs. Rumproast realized that the room was also filled with a nasty, nasty smell.

"Ewww!" yelled Mr. Rumproast. "What crawled up inside of you and died?"

"Today at school they served beans for lunch None of the other students wanted any, so I ate the entire pot," answered Stanley.

"It was a 10-gallon pot," added Arthur.

"He's flatulent!" said Mrs. Rumproast, having just opened the bedroom window as much as it would open.

"Flat-you-what?" asked Arthur.

Mrs. Rumproast tried to explain. "He's gassy, uh, colicky..."

"She means I can't stop farting," said Stanley as he again broke wind and with a long "Frrpppt!" rose three feet off the bed.

"What can we do?" Said Mr. Rumproast.

"I know what I'm going to do," said Arthur. "As long as Stanley keeps cutting the cheese, I'm going to sleep in the living room! Pew!"

And for once, Arthur's parents agreed with him.

THE STUDENTS GET WIND OF STANLEY

On the first day back at school after Stanley ate the big pot of beans, the other students could sense there was something different in the air, even before Stanley arrived.

"Do you smell something funny?" asked Trevor. "Yes, it smells like a big clog at the sewage plant," said Jasmine.

"Look!" shouted Benjamin, as he pointed down the street. All the students saw what he was pointing at: Stanley could be seen rising up above the trees, lifted by what looked like a greenish-brown cloud. When Stanley and Arthur arrived in the school yard, all the students surrounded him — at first.

"Stanley, why were you floating in the air?" asked Stephan. "I'm flatulent," answered Stanley, as his parents had instructed him to do.

"Flat WHAT?" said Tom. "I think that means he makes smelly blurps" said Emily. "No," interrupted Trevor, "it means he fires off air biscuits." Benjamin said, "Stanley means he has belly bombs." "You know what Stanley has now?" riddled Jasmine. "A butt bugle!"

"What he means," said Arthur, "is that he farts. Big."

Just then, Stanley went "Fraffffft!" and raised several feet above the schoolyard. All the students ran away screaming, choking and holding their noses. Stanley had just learned another new word: unpopular.

STANLEY'S BIG TEST

When class started, Stanley sat on one side of the room and all the other students sat on the other side of the room, in case Stanley cut a big ripper.

Just then, the teacher, Mrs. Toomey, entered the room. "Class, today I'm giving you a surprise 100-question quiz." The students moaned as Mrs. Toomey began handing out the test papers.

Suddenly, Stanley had an idea. None of the

teachers knew yet that he was now Flatulent Stanley.

After putting his finger to his mouth to warn the other students to be quiet, he pushed against the back of his seat and released a huge silent-but-deadly cloud.

"What's that foul smell?" asked Mrs. Toomey. "It smells like the gas pipes might be leaking," said Benjamin, playing along with Stanley.

"Eww! It smells like an explosion at the sauerkraut factory!" said Mrs. Toomey. "Class, line up and leave the school, I'm reporting this to the Principal!"

Mrs. Toomey told the Principal, who also smelled the foul, gassy cloud. Together they spoke to all the students, now lined up outside the school. "I'm sorry, but until we find out what the

smell is, I won't be able to give the quiz," said Mr Toomey. "In fact, it smells so bad in there I'm calling off school for the rest of the day," added the Principal. As the students ran home, a cheer went up. Stanley, you're the hero of the whole school," said Emily. With another cheer, the students raised Stanley and began carrying him on their shoulders. That ended one loud "Fuurrrt!" later.

ALES FROM THE DUCK SIDE DEPT.

THE ROTTEN ROYAL RUSE

Your Majesty! You can't RAISE the TAXES again! Your subjects are so poor that many have taken to the streets to beg!
NONSENSE! You make it out to be WORSE than it is! I will GO OUT and see for MYSELF what they think of their KING!

But, Sire! THINK of the DANGER!
Don't be a FOOL! I will be DISGUISED as one of their own! They will NEVER KNOW their KING walks AMONG THEM!

YOUR HIGHNESS! Your DISGUISE is AMAZING! If I didn't know you to be the KING, I'd believe you to be a BEGGAR in the STREETS!
HAH! If YOU can be CONVINCED Gunther, then surely no lowly BEGGAR will SUSPECT my TRUE IDENTITY! Please get my HAT!

WRITER AND ARTIST: DUCK EDWING

HEY, guys! I really do LOVE our KING! WHAT do YOU THINK about HIM?
PLEASE

ARE A S

Are you lacking a little in the personal hygiene department? Do you take a bath once a month, whether you think you need it or not? Has a government agency ever ordered the evacuation of your room fearing a massive "junk avalanche?" Then perhaps you should spend the next few minutes taking the following MAD quiz...

You start with 100 points. Add additional points after each question.

1) For every slice of pizza your mother finds when she makes your bed .... **ADD 3**

2) If your mother has to use an ice scraper your clothes before washing them....**ADD**
A jackhammer..............................**ADD**

3) For every pet who has ever "gone missing" in your room **ADD 20**

4) If the pile of dirty laundry in your room joined the Great Wall of China and the Pyramids as the only man-made objects visible from space **ADD 10**

5) If, when having a sleepover, your friend' parents insist on them wearing bio-hazard s before entering your room................**ADD**

YOU LOB?

WRITER: J. PRETE
ARTIST: JOHNNY RYAN

7) If you can write your name in the dust on your furniture........**ADD 5**

If you can write the name of every kid in your class..........**ADD 10**

Every kid in your school...........**ADD 20**

6) If your room was near the center of a massive earthquake and mudslide, and it looked the same after the quake was over..........**ADD 10**

8) If there is enough dirt under your fingernails to grow a small tomato plant **ADD 5**

) If you put on a clean shirt very morning..................**ADD 0**

you put on the shirt that tinks the least..............**ADD 5**

the question doesn't apply to you ecause you usually wear the same lothes you slept in......**ADD 10**

10) If you spent an hour rooting through all your junk trying to find a pencil to take this test **ADD 10**

If you scored more than 115, you're a real super slob!
If you scored less than 115, you're a regular slob!
Either way, you're a slob!

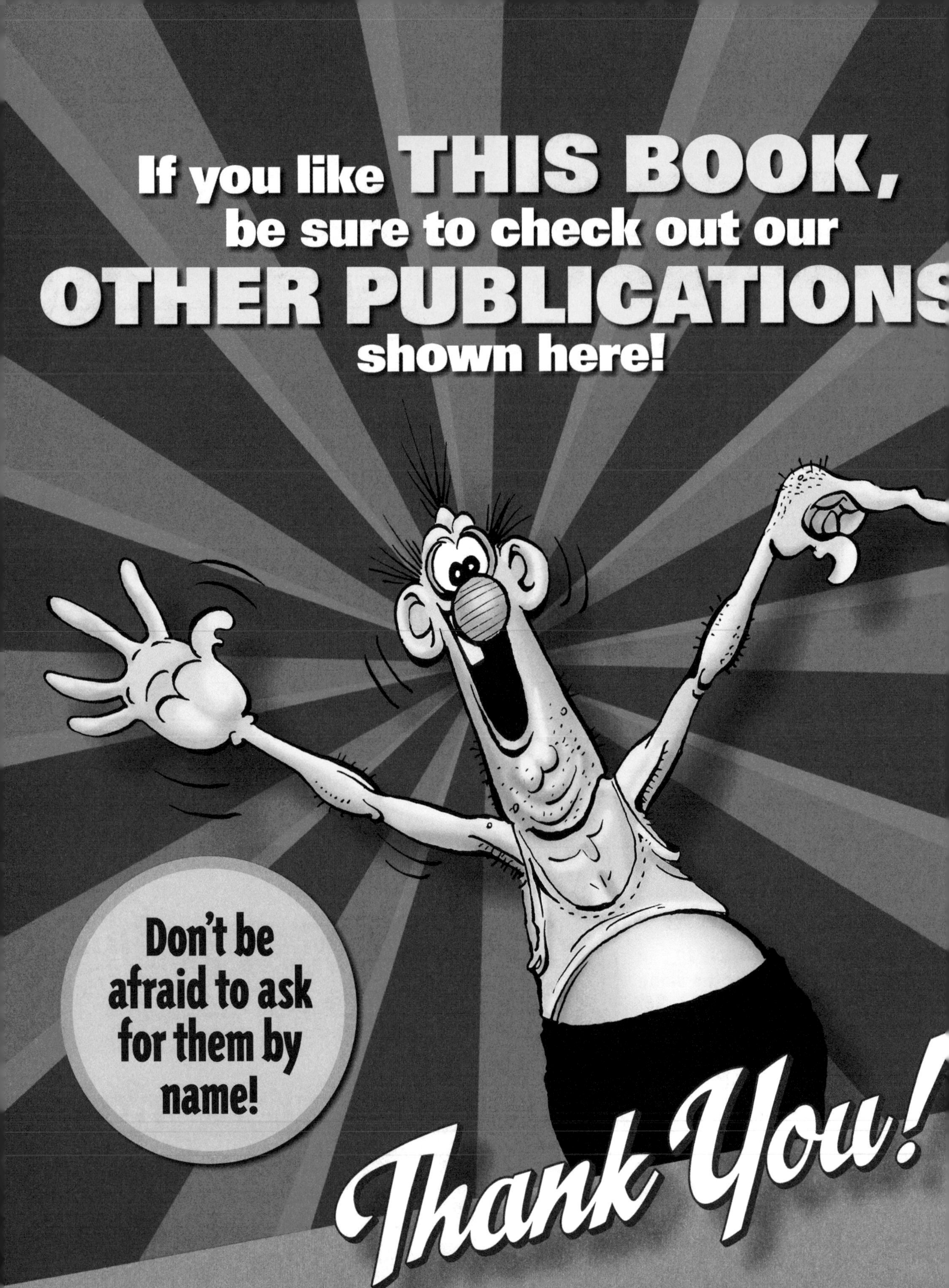

Don't be afraid to ask for them by name!

Thank You!

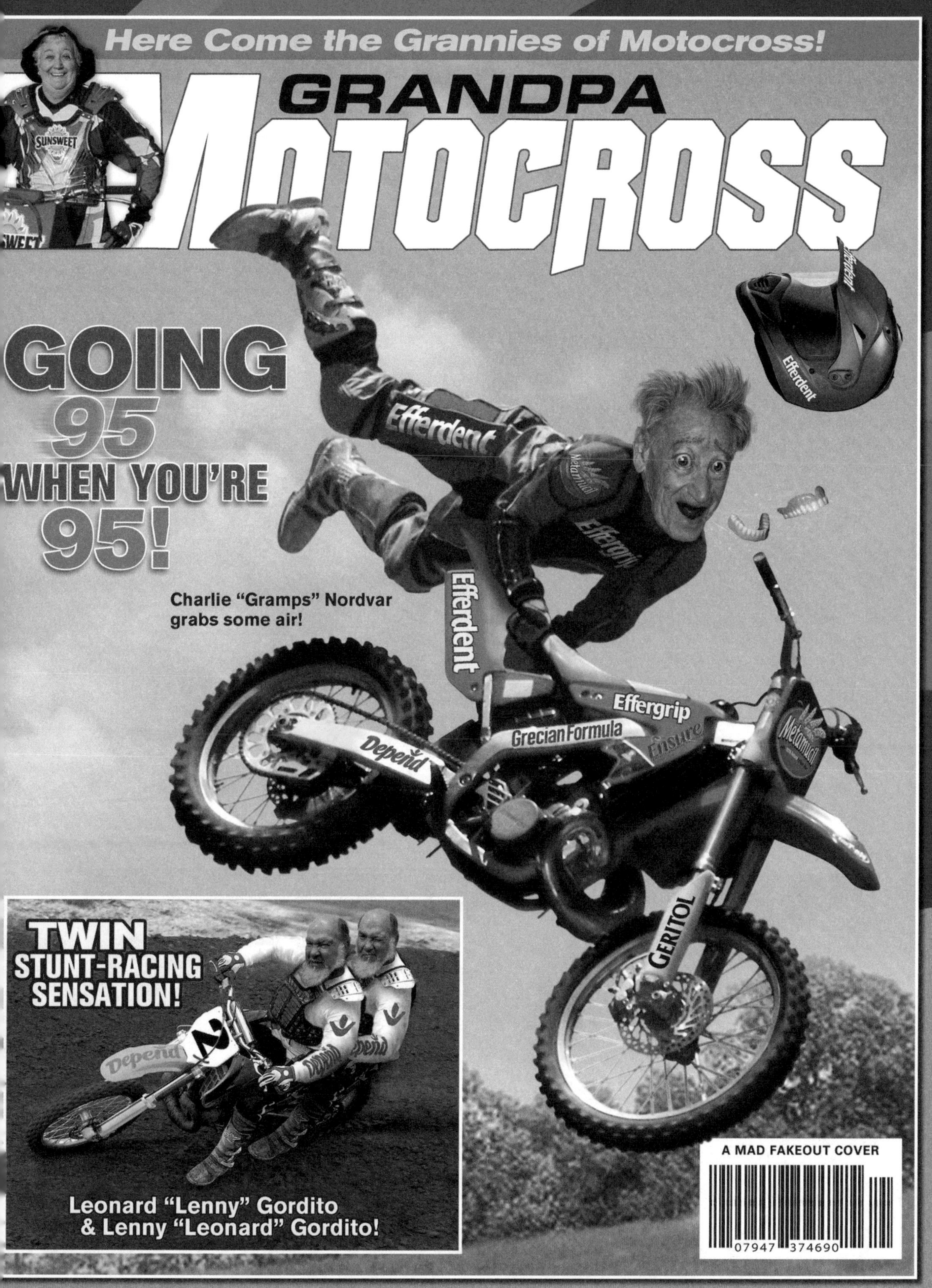
Here Come the Grannies of Motocross!
GRANDPA
MOTOCROSS
GOING
95
WHEN YOU'RE
95!
Charlie "Gramps" Nordvar
grabs some air!
TWIN
STUNT-RACING
SENSATION!
Leonard "Lenny" Gordito
& Lenny "Leonard" Gordito!
A MAD FAKEOUT COVER
07947 374690
SUNSWEET
Efferdent
Effergrip
Metamucil
Depend
Grecian Formula
Ensure
GERITOL

Jockey Overboard
A True Story

Boating For Horses

MARCH 2012

We Test Drive the Newest Powerboats!

Saying "Whoa!" to Seasickness

"Row, Row, Row Your Oats" & 7 Other Delightful Sea Chanteys

Getting Shoed for Water-skis

>>> NEW HEAD LICE MERIT BADGE PLANNED SEE PAGE 9

Boys' Lice

WHERE SCOUTING AND INFESTATION MEET

TURN YOUR HEAD INTO A HATCHERY...

...IT'S EASY!

PAGE 22

Training your nits to do TRICKS!

Share hats with your friends and have a LICE DAY!

$3.60

A MAD FAKEOUT COVER

DON MARTIN DEPT.

DON MARTIN BEATS TH

HIGH COST OF GASOLINE

WRITER AND ARTIST: DON MARTIN

WATER
AIR COND.

WATER
KLIK
VROOM
SPOOSH

WATER

MARBLE SHOOTING CHAMPIONSHIP

SPRAY CANS MADE TO ORDER

PSSSH

BIRD VITAMINS

D.MARTIN..